# THE RIGHT TO

# RESIST

## Zionism and Fascism

## Hichem Karoui

Global East–West for Studies and Publishing

# CONTENTS

# THE RIGHT TO

# RESIST

Zionism and Fascism

## Hichem Karoui

Global East-West for Studies and Publishing

# About This Collection: Resistances

In this compelling and thought-provoking collection of books labelled "Resistances," produced by GEW Reports & Analyses, we embark on an immersive voyage through the rich tapestry of history, unveiling the heroic narratives of movements that steadfastly resisted the waves of oppression, colonisation, and exploitation. Beyond being a mere historical account, this collection is a tribute to the unbreakable spirit of resistance reverberating across the globe — from the bustling streets of North Africa and the Middle East to the far corners where Buddhist and Marxist ideologies intertwined with the quest for emancipation.

Each volume within this collection is a dedicated exploration of a distinct nation: Tunisia, Algeria, Morocco, Egypt, Sudan, Syria, Iraq, Lebanon, but also the USA (civil rights struggle), China (100 years of humiliation), South Africa ( Apartheid), Vietnam, Indochina, India, among others, delving deeply into their distinctive struggles against a shared antagonist — the imperialist West. The narrative transcends conflicts; it offers an illuminating journey into how ideologies such as Islam, Marxism, and Buddhism have acted as catalysts and guiding philosophies for these remarkable movements.

This collection's heart lies in the enduring struggle in Palestine, set against a broader historical and geopolitical canvas backdrop. The Palestinian resistance against Israeli occupation, depicted here as an extension of Western imperialism, is presented with profound insight and perspective, challenging conventional narratives. This collection fearlessly confronts the dissonance between the West's professed ideals of democracy and human rights and its actions, often at odds with these principles.

"Resistances" serves a dual purpose. Firstly, it serves as an educational beacon, enlightening younger generations about the often unspoken stories of people living under the yoke of colonisation and their relentless pursuit of freedom. Secondly, it seeks to shed light on the injustices perpetrated by Western powers, offering a critical examination of their support for expansionist and oppressive policies while categorising those who resist as 'terrorists', despite international law recognising the right to resist occupation.

Is Hamas and other Palestinian organisations that resist the military occupation "terrorist" organisations? No, they are not. The United Nations General Assembly (UNGA) has explicitly affirmed the right of Palestinians to resist Israel's military occupation, *including through armed struggle*. This right was affirmed in the context of the right to self-determination of all peoples under foreign and colonial rule. Some of the most relevant UN resolutions on this matter include:

- UNGA Resolution 3314 (1974) affirmed the right of self-determination, freedom, and independence for all "peoples under colonial and racist regimes or other forms of alien domination." It affirmed the "right of these peoples to struggle to that end and to seek and receive support."[1]

- UNGA Resolution 37/43 (1982) reaffirmed the "inalienable right" of the Palestinian people "and all peoples under foreign and colonial domination" to self-determination. It also reiterates the legitimacy of "the struggle of peoples for [...] liberation from colonial and foreign domination and foreign occupation by all available means, including armed struggle."[2]

Similar principles have been repeated in numerous other UNGA resolutions. Although UNGA resolutions are not legally binding, they "accurately reflect the customary international legal opinion among the majority of the world's sovereign states."[3]

In international law, the right to resist is closely related to the principle of self-determination. It is widely recognised that a right to self-determination arises in situations of colonial domination, foreign occupation, and racist regimes that deny a segment of the population political participation. All this applies to the Israeli occupation of Palestine.

For instance, international law legitimises Palestinian attempts to resist Israeli oppression [4]. The International Bill of Human Rights also implicitly teaches the right to resist oppression. The preamble to the Universal Declaration of Human Rights states that it is essential for human rights to be protected by the rule of law to prevent individuals from resorting to rebellion against tyranny and oppression [5].

Anti-colonial movements, a form of resistance against colonial rule, have been instrumental in the struggle for self-determination in colonised countries (Tunisia, Algeria, Egypt, Sudan, China, Vietnam, etc.) These movements have often been concerned with the world that decolonised nations were to inherit collectively[6].

The right to resist oppression and colonisation is a fundamental human right recognised in international law and human rights instruments. Nothing could change this fact, even if the USA and Europe, still clinging to their old imperialist traditions, stand alone on the planet against the Right to Resist until the end of times.

This collection is a testament to the indomitable human spirit and the unwavering quest for freedom and justice. It is a scholarly opus, meticulously researched and presented. Yet, it is also a narrative that speaks to the soul, serving as a reminder of the universal values of liberty and dignity. As the editor and publisher, I am honoured to introduce this "Resistances" collection, firmly believing that it will inspire our readers, encouraging them to view history and contemporary events through a lens of nuanced comprehension and empathy.

We extend a warm invitation to embark on this extraordinary journey through "Resistances," where you will uncover the hitherto untold tales of courage, resilience, and the relentless pursuit of justice that have profoundly shaped our world.

Hichem Karoui

Senior Researcher and Editor of the "Resistances" collection.

London, 24 November 2023

1. UNGA resolution 3314, "Definition of Aggression," December 14, 1974.

2. UNGA resolution 37/43, "Importance of the universal realization of the right of peoples to self-determination and of the speedy granting of independence to colonial countries and peoples for the effective guarantee and observance of human rights," December 3, 1982.

3. John Sigler, "Palestine: Legitimate Armed Resistance vs. Terrorism," *Electronic Intifada,* May 17 2004.

4. Werleman, Cj. "International Law Guarantees Palestinians the Right to Resist." International law guarantees Palestinians the right to resist, May 28, 2018. https://www.trtworld.com/opinion/international-law-g

uarantees-palestinians-the-right-to-resist-17810.

5. United Nations. "Universal Declaration of Human Rights | United Nations," n.d. https://www.un.org/en/about-us/univer sal-declaration-of-human-rights.

6. Elam, J. Daniel. Global South Studies, U.Va. "Anticolonialism," n.d. https://globalsouthstudies.as.virginia.edu/key-concepts/an ticolonialism.

# Dedication

To the people of Gaza who never gave up to the occupation.
To the Palestinian people fighting the most horrid colonisation. To the children of Palestine assassinated by the cowers,
who keep coming back from death to stone the fascists. To
their heroic mothers and sisters. To all the women and men
of Palestine who show daily how strong they are. To all those
who fight with their hands, the soldiers of an Apartheid fascist system imposed and supported by a hypocritical imperialist West. To all those who still resist fascism and Zionist colonialism in Palestine and elsewhere, often with bare
hands, faith and goodwill. To the martyrs of the Palestinian
cause. To all those who have faith that the right of return to
the ancestral land will never disappear. Palestine shall, sooner
or later, be liberated.

# EPIGRAPHS

There is no peace possible with Fascism.

"Those who can make you believe absurdities, can make you commit atrocities." - Voltaire

"In the End, we will remember not the words of our enemies, but the silence of our friends." - Martin Luther King Jr.

# Book One: Brief History Of Resistance As Idea And Action

# PRELUDE

I n the world of resistance, individuals and communities rise against injustice, oppression, and tyranny. Throughout history, resistance has played a vital and transformative role in shaping societies, challenging the status quo, and advocating for change. From ancient civilisations to the modern era, acts of resistance have sparked revolutions, inspired social movements, and forever changed the course of human history.

## The Seeds of Resistance in Ancient Civilisations

Our exploration begins in the early days of humanity, where the seeds of resistance were sown in the fertile ground of ancient civilisations. In ancient Egypt, the construction of monumental structures such as the Great Pyramids often relied on a labour force of peasants and workers who, at times, staged strikes or walkouts to express their discontent and demand better working conditions. These demonstrations of solidarity and collective action exemplify the power of unity in resisting oppressive regimes.

Moving further in time, we encounter the ancient Greek city-states, renowned for their contributions to the foundations of modern democracy. Here, resistance took on a philosophical dimension. Figures such as

Socrates, who challenged conventional beliefs and questioned the authority of the Athenian state, faced persecution and ultimately chose death over capitulation. Their intellectual resistance, rooted in the pursuit of truth, reason, and individual autonomy, inspired generations to question and challenge prevailing norms and societal structures.

## Feudalism and Peasant Uprisings:

Transitioning to the medieval period, we find ourselves in an era dominated by feudalism – an economic and social system marked by a stark division of power and wealth. In this system, peasants toiled under the dominion of feudal lords, enduring heavy burdens and oppressive conditions. However, resistance was not extinguished. Peasant uprisings, such as the Jacquerie in the 14th century France and the German Peasants' War in the 16th century, exemplified the determination of the oppressed classes to challenge the feudal order and dismantle the system that perpetuated their suffering. These movements were characterised by demands for fair treatment, abolishing serfdom, and a more equitable distribution of land and resources.

## The Enlightenment and the Intellectual Rebellion:

As Europe transitioned from the feudal age to the Enlightenment, resistance took on new forms and found its voice in intellectual rebellion. The Enlightenment brought forth a philosophical movement that challenged traditional authority and extolled the virtues of reason, knowledge, and individual rights. Prominent thinkers such as John Locke, Voltaire, and Jean-Jacques Rousseau disseminated ideas that questioned the legitimacy of absolutist monarchies and advocated for establishing more representative and accountable forms of governance. Their writings served as a call to arms for resistance against oppressive regimes, paving the way for democratic revolutions in the late 18th and early 19th centuries.

## Age of Revolutions and Nationalism:

The dawn of the 19th century marked a period of radical change as waves of nationalism surged across Europe and the Americas. Resistance movements took centre stage as people sought to reclaim their cultural identities and assert their desires for self-governance. The American Revolution, fuelled by a commitment to the principles of liberty and self-determination, severed ties with British colonial rule and established a new democratic republic. Similarly, the French Revolution, ignited by equality, fraternity, and liberty ideals, saw the French people overthrow the monarchy and set in motion a new era of extraordinary political and social changes.

In addition to these seminal events, numerous uprisings unfolded across Europe during this era, driven by a potent blend of nationalist fervour, economic grievances, and demands for social justice. The Hungarian Revolution of 1848, the Greek War of Independence, and the various uprisings against oppressive colonial rule in Latin America demonstrate the immense power of collective resistance in dismantling oppressive systems and ushering in new eras of independence and social progress.

## Colonial Resistance and Struggles for Independence:

The colonial era witnessed resistance taking on a new dimension as indigenous populations, subjected to centuries of colonial rule, began to challenge the oppressive yoke of foreign powers. The struggle for independence became a battle for sovereignty, cultural preservation, and the rejection of the dehumanising effects of colonisation. The Haitian Revolution (1791-1804) stands as a remarkable testament to resistance. Born out of the enduring spirit of freedom and the desire for emancipation, enslaved Africans and their allies rose against the powerful French empire, successfully establishing the first nation in the Western Hemisphere led by former slaves.

Similar resistance movements birthed national independence across Latin America, as revolutionary leaders such as Simón Bolívar and José de San Martín led campaigns against colonial powers, toppling oppressive regimes and forging new nations. In Asia, the Indian subcontinent witnessed the valiant resistance of figures like Mahatma Gandhi, who advocated for nonviolent means of resistance against British colonial rule. Through civil disobedience, boycotts, and nonviolent protests, they challenged the moral authority of the oppressor and secured independence for their respective nations.


## World Wars and Occupations:


The early 20th century brought unprecedented challenges as the world was consumed by two devastating world wars and the occupation of entire nations. Against this backdrop, resistance took on diverse and resilient forms. Occupied countries experienced the emergence of underground networks and partisan warfare as resistance fighters courageously engaged in sabotage, espionage, and acts of sabotage against occupying forces. These clandestine efforts served to preserve national identity and disrupt the oppressor's grip.

The bravery of individuals and communities during this period is exemplified by the French Resistance, who defiantly resisted Nazi occupation through clandestine activities and acts of sabotage. The Warsaw Uprising, a valiant but ill-fated rebellion by the Polish Home Army against Nazi forces, stands as a testament to the indomitable spirit of those who refused to surrender their dignity and freedom.

## Beyond Ideological Divides:

In the aftermath of World War II, the world became polarised by competing political ideologies during the Cold War. Resistance movements operating within countries under totalitarian regimes waged a battle for human rights, freedom of expression, and self-determination. The Solidarity movement in Poland, led by Lech Walesa, exemplifies the power of solidarity, as workers and intellectuals joined forces in a nonviolent struggle against the communist regime. Their collective resistance ultimately led to the fall of the Iron Curtain and the dismantling of oppressive systems in Eastern Europe.

The United States witnessed a powerful civil rights movement in the mid-20th century, as African Americans and their allies resisted racial segregation and demanded equal rights. Led by figures such as Martin Luther King Jr., Rosa Parks, and Malcolm X, these nonviolent resistance efforts brought attention to the systemic racial injustices faced by African Americans. They paved the way for significant legal and social reforms.

Simultaneously, the feminist movement emerged on a global scale, calling for gender equality and challenging patriarchal structures across societies. Women's rights activists raised their voices against discrimination, wage disparities, and the denial of basic rights. The struggle for gender equality proved to be a powerful force for change, reshaping societal norms and galvanising diverse movements for women's rights worldwide.

## The Digital Age and Evolving Forms of Resistance:

With the advent of the digital age, resistance found new avenues of expression and mobilisation. Digital platforms and social media networks have become powerful tools for organising and amplifying voices of resistance. Movements such as the Arab Spring in the early 2010s highlighted the ability of ordinary individuals to come together, coordinate actions, and challenge oppressive regimes through the use of social media platforms. Activists used technology to share information, raise awareness, and mobilise mass demonstrations, leading to significant political upheaval in countries such as Egypt, Tunisia, and Syria.

In addition to digital platforms, art and culture have also emerged as potent forms of resistance in the modern era. Artists and creatives have used their work to challenge social norms, provoke thought, and spark conversations about pressing issues. Whether through visual art, music, performance, or literature, culture can inspire, unite, and instigate change.

Furthermore, resistance is not limited to specific periods or geographical locations. It is a perennial force that continues to shape our world today. From the fight against racial injustice and police brutality to the struggle for Palestinian rights to the battle against climate change, resistance movements persist and evolve.

## Conclusion:

Resistance is a thread that weaves through the tapestry of human history, connecting struggles and movements across time and space. From ancient civilisations to this day, resistance has been a catalyst for change, enabling individuals and communities to challenge oppression, defy unjust systems, and fight for a better future. The stories of resistance remind us of the power of collective action, the strength of the human spirit, and the enduring desire for freedom, justice, and equality. As we examine these narratives of resistance, we are encouraged to reflect upon our roles in shaping a more just and equitable world.

# ANCIENT CIVILISATIONS AND THE BIRTH OF RESISTANCE

R esistance has been a constant companion throughout the vast expanse of human history, a thread intricately woven through the ages. We find not just traces but flourishing examples of defiance against oppressive rulers and unjust systems, even in the earliest civilisations. Exploring the origins of resistance in the annals of ancient history is a journey that unfolds like a mesmerising epic, filled with tales of bravery and unwavering determination.

One of the earliest examples of resistance can be found in Mesopotamia, also known as the "Cradle of Civilisation." The Sumerians, the forefathers of human civilisation, boldly rebelled against their rulers here. As early as 2350 BCE, the Sumerian city-states revolted against Sargon of Akkad's hegemony, which sought to centralise power and impose his authority with an iron fist. The Sumerian King List, an ancient chronicle etched on clay tablets, also reveals numerous instances where city-states valiantly resisted foreign dominance over the centuries.

However, resistance in ancient Mesopotamia was not limited to political rebellion. The Sumerians, known for their advanced civilisation, expressed their resistance through the lyrical beauty of their literary works. The renowned "Lament for Ur," a Sumerian poem that mourns the tragic fall of the majestic city of Ur to the marauding Elamites, is one such example that has stood the test of time. The Sumerians expressed not only their sorrow but also their indomitable spirit of defiance, refusing to let the flames of their culture die out. Indeed, preserving their culture was an act of resistance in and of itself, a determined effort to preserve their identity amid conquest's tumultuous chaos.

Ancient Egypt, steeped in the grandeur of its pharaohs, witnessed acts of resistance, especially during the reigns of those mighty rulers. The time-less story of Moses leading the Hebrews out of Egypt is a testament to the power of resistance. Shackled by the chains of slavery and oppressed by Pharaoh's tyranny, the Israelites dared to confront their oppressors' colossal might. While the story contains mythical elements, it serves as an indelible reminder of the unwavering spirit of resistance against tyranny that prevailed even in ancient history's hallowed corridors. The Israelites' resistance was not limited to a physical struggle for liberation; it embodied a profound spiritual and cultural rebellion against their oppressors' yoke, a hymn of defiance that echoed through the sands of time.

When we look at ancient Greece, we see a society that was celebrated for its democratic ideals but where resistance flourished. Greek city-states rose in unison within this progressive civilisation, a symphony of defiance against the spectre of tyrannical rulers, their voices harmonising in the pursuit of preserving their democratic traditions. The Athenian resistance against the formidable Persians during the tumultuous Greco-Persian Wars is perhaps the most celebrated of these episodes. The very essence of democracy was intertwined with the spirit of resistance here. The Greek city-states, united by their fervent love of freedom and unyielding thirst for autonomy, took up arms against overwhelming odds to defend their cherished way of life, etching their collective determination into the annals of history and providing an enduring wellspring of inspiration for future generations of resistance movements.

However, resistance in ancient Greece went beyond mere political revolts. The philosophical schools that flourished during this golden age, such as the Cynics, Stoics, and Epicureans, can be seen as intellectual resistance movements. Thinkers like Diogenes of Sinope, Zeno of Citium, and Epicurus emerged as intellectual rebels. They dared to question societal norms, to question rulers' unchecked authority, and to advocate for a virtuous life free of external constraints. Their teachings echoed themes of personal freedom, self-reliance, and the never-ending pursuit of happiness, providing individuals with an alternative way to resist the shackles of social injustice and oppression.

In the context of ancient Rome, the establishment of the Roman Republic opened up avenues for resistance to oppressive aristocrats and would-be dictators. Shakespeare's dramatic portrayal of Julius Caesar's assassination by a group of senators, immortalised in history, can be seen as a poignant act of resistance against his burgeoning autocratic tendencies. During Rome's transition from a republic to an empire, subjugated peoples staged numerous uprisings, each motivated by a strong desire to reclaim their freedom and assert their rights. The Jewish revolts against Roman rule, particularly the First and Second Jewish Revolts, stand out as significant chapters in the history of resistance, fuelled by a complex mix of religious zeal, nationalism, and socio-political motivations.

Nonetheless, the tapestry of resistance stretches far beyond the borders of Mesopotamia, Egypt, Greece, and Rome. Throughout human history, resistance has emerged in various civilisations worldwide. History presents a rich mosaic of resistance against exploitation and tyranny, from indigenous tribes in the Americas who valiantly resisted the tide of European colonisation to ancient Chinese peasants who rose in defiance against oppressive feudal lords. The Mayan resistance to the juggernaut of Spanish conquest, the Tamil resistance to Chola imperialism in the sun-kissed lands of South India, and the Carthaginian defiance of Rome's relentless expansionist ambitions—all of these instances exemplify the indomitable human spirit that yearned for liberation, self-determination, and justice.

The emergence of resistance in these ancient civilisations was not limited to armed uprisings. Philosophers and thinkers emerged as a formidable force, challenging dominant ideologies and championing the cause of social transformation. Confucius' teachings in ancient China, as well as the revolutionary ideas of ancient Indian philosophers such as Buddha and Mahavira, are shining examples of resistance through the power of intellectual discourse. These visionary minds dared to challenge societal norms, scrutinised existing power structures, and presented alternative visions for a just and harmonious society.

Understanding the origins of resistance in these ancient civilisations provides us with profound insights into the seeds of dissent sown throughout human history. It is a lasting reminder that the fervent desire for freedom, justice, and autonomy is an intrinsic aspect of the human spirit. This timeless yearning has transcended time and space. These ancient acts of resistance paved the way for future generations to challenge oppressive systems and ardently strive for a better world, inspiring individuals to rise valiantly against adversity and carry the torch of resistance forward through time.

# The Middle Ages: Religion and Resistance

During the medieval era, religion wielded an all-encompassing influence over societal affairs, exerting profound sway over politics, social dynamics, and intellectual discourse. Nevertheless, not all individuals submitted unquestioningly to this ecclesiastical dominion. Instead, they charted a course of resistance, mounting formidable challenges to the prevailing religious orthodoxy and endeavouring to redefine the intricate interplay between individuals and institutional entities.

Heresy emerged as one of the earliest manifestations of religious resistance during the medieval epoch. Heretical movements arose as dissenting voices vehemently opposed the teachings and practises sanctioned by the Catholic Church. For instance, consider the Cathars inhabiting the lush landscapes of southern France. They espoused a dualistic cosmology, contending that the material realm bore the imprints of diabolical creation. Consequently, they spurned numerous Catholic sacraments and rituals, ardently advocating for a more streamlined, spiritually-infused expression of Christianity.

Similarly, in the northern reaches of Italy, the Waldensians mounted a vociferous critique of the Church's opulent riches and hierarchical structure, exalting the virtues of austerity, humility, and the profound significance of direct engagement with scriptural texts. These disparate heretical movements precipitated a direct challenge to the ecclesiastical hegemony of the Catholic Church and its monopolistic control over theological interpretation. In response, ecclesiastical authorities orchestrated the establishment of the Inquisition, a religious tribunal singularly dedicated to the identification, prosecution, and eradication of heretical tendencies.

The arsenal of the Inquisition encompassed an assortment of methodologies, including the harrowing practice of torture and the public spectacle of burnings at the stake, all meticulously engineered to stifle dissent and perpetuate the Church's dominance. Nevertheless, despite the relentless endeavours devoted to this enterprise, heretical movements persisted, leaving an indelible mark on the tapestry of Europe's religious landscape. One notable instance of religious resistance during the medieval epoch was the Protestant Reformation, a transformative phenomenon reverberating across both the religious and political realms. The genesis of this epoch-defining movement can be traced to the indomitable spirit of Martin Luther, a dedicated Augustinian monk whose efforts commenced in 1517.

Luther directed his formidable intellectual prowess toward critiquing the sale of indulgences, contending that the salvation of souls rested solely on unwavering faith, untouched by the commercialisation of divine clemency. His Ninety-Five Theses swiftly ascended to the forefront of theological discourse, effectively kindling a conflagration of unparalleled intellectual enquiry and reformist fervour.

However, Luther's polemical disquisitions transcended the confines of his initial critique, assuming the form of a multifaceted assault on various foundational tenets and practises endorsed by the Catholic Church. His interrogation of the Pope's ecclesiastical authority, emphasis on the universal priesthood of believers, and impassioned plea for individualised in-

terpretations of scriptural texts ignited spirited debates. The advent of Jo-
hannes Gutenberg's revolutionary invention, the printing press, expedited
the dissemination of Luther's ideas, propelling them across the European
continent with unparallelled velocity, thereby engendering spirited debates
and kindling the collective fervour for reform.

The Protestant Reformation gave birth to an eclectic array of Protestant denominations, each characterised by its unique theological predis-
positions and modes of resistance vis-à-vis the Catholic Church. Take,
for example, the ecclesiastical landscape of Geneva, presided over by the
indomitable John Calvin, who extolled the doctrine of predestination and
envisioned a harmonious Christian society governed by the imperatives
of religious rectitude. In contrast, consider the milieu of Zurich, where
Huldrych Zwingli spearheaded a theological paradigm shift, advocating
for a symbolic interpretation of the Eucharist while soundly rejecting
transubstantiation. These eminent reformers, among an illustrious pantheon of others, broadened the horizons of Protestantism, thus propelling
a vibrant diversity of religious ideologies into the crucible of European
religious discourse, thereby catalysing an epoch marked by the coexistence
and contestation of multiple religious paradigms.

However, the dissemination of Protestant ideas ignited a conflagration
of religious wars and internecine conflicts that sundered the fabric of
societies across the continent. The German Peasants' War, a confluence
of socio-economic grievances and simmering religious discontent, erupted
in the early 16th century, resulting in widespread insurrections against
feudal overlords and ecclesiastical holdings. After that, France was torn
apart by the long-lasting Wars of Religion, which happened over several
decades and involved Catholics and Protestants fighting among themselves
for power, causing terrible deaths and unimaginable damage.

The annals of history reveal a profound interplay between political
machinations and religious resistance during the medieval epoch, as secular
rulers artfully navigated the intricate labyrinth of ecclesiastical authority.
The Investiture Controversy, an epochal conflict that unfolded during the
late 11th and early 12th centuries, embroiled the Holy Roman Empire

and the papal seat in an intractable struggle for supremacy in ecclesiastical appointments. Secular potentates, including the enigmatic Henry VIII of England, astutely discerned the potential of harnessing religious resistance as a potent tool to secure their autonomy and consolidate their spheres of influence.

The rupture of Henry VIII's association with Rome and the subsequent establishment of the Church of England stand as indelible testaments to how political imperatives intermeshed with the currents of religious resistance, ultimately shaping the course of history.

The annals of the Middle Ages bear witness to innumerable instances of resistance against religious conventions and institutional norms, reflecting the multifaceted tapestry of medieval society. From heretical movements that castigated the Church's authority to the Protestant Reformation that catalysed a profound transformation of European Christendom to the intricate power struggles that unfurled between ecclesiastical authorities and secular rulers, the medieval epoch served as an incendiary crucible of religious and political metamorphosis.

The legacy of these acts of resistance continues to animate our comprehension of religiosity, the dynamics of power, and the intricate interplay between individual agency and the edifices of institutional authority. They serve as a poignant reminder that the quest for religious autonomy and the reform of ecclesiastical institutions are perennial pursuits that demand incessant critical scrutiny and contemplation, even when confronted with the inexorable march of adversity.

# The Enlightenment Era: Resistance as Intellectual Rebellion

During the epoch known as the Enlightenment, a fresh wave of resistance arose, a period spanning the 17th and 18th centuries that bore witness to a profound transformation in thought. This era was marked by a remarkable shift in intellectual paradigms that exalted reason while harbouring a streak of scepticism and a burgeoning devotion to individualism. Within this chronological sphere, luminaries embarked upon the formidable endeavour of challenging the conventions of their day, the established authorities, and the oppressive systems that held sway. Their chosen arsenal consisted of ideas and the written word, as they aspired to liberate society from the shackles of ignorance, superstition, and the dogmatic tenets of religion. It is imperative to acknowledge that the resistance mounted by these Enlightenment intellectuals transcended mere political symbolism; at its core, it represented an intellectual odyssey to reconstruct society through the propagation of rationality, critical thought, and the ideals of egalitarianism.

Among the eminent figures of this era, one encounters Voltaire, the French philosopher and scribe who, under the birth name François-Marie Arouet, etched an indelible imprint upon the intellectual landscape. Voltaire's literary oeuvre was pivotal in advocating for religious tolerance, freedom of expression, and the unequivocal demarcation between church and state. Born in 1694, Voltaire bore witness to the stark realities and flagrant hypocrisies that the Catholic Church, monarchy, and aristocracy perpetuated. His campaign against religious intolerance and his trenchant critiques of corrupt institutions marked him for censorship and persecution. He endured imprisonment on two occasions and eventual exile, yet he refused to be silenced. His literary compositions, including the celebrated opus "Candide," probed the inequities and power abuses that pervaded society, all while issuing a clarion call for realising a more equitable and enlightened world. Voltaire's unwavering commitment to the pursuit of veracity and justice solidified his status as an emblem of resistance against tyranny.

Another towering luminary of this epoch was Jean-Jacques Rousseau, the Swiss-French philosopher and litterateur whose birth occurred in 1712. Rousseau embarked upon a formidable crusade against the established social and political orders of his era through his pioneering treatises on social contract theory and the inherent natural rights of individuals. In his seminal work, "The Social Contract," Rousseau posited that true political legitimacy could only emanate from the consensus of the governed, espousing the need for a government firmly rooted in the sovereignty of the populace. He levelled scathing censure against the absolute monarchy, advocating instead for a more egalitarian societal framework in which individual liberty coexisted harmoniously with the broader interests of the general will. His emphasis on the primacy of the general will and the promulgation of the common good served as a wellspring of inspiration for revolutionary movements and played a pivotal role in establishing republican forms of governance. The Enlightenment epoch also bore witness to the efflorescence of salon culture, wherein writers, thinkers, and intellectuals convened within the confines of private residences to engage in spirited and erudite intellectual discourse. These salons functioned as vibrant hubs of resistance, furnishing a platform for exchanging radical ideas and serving as a potent counterpoint to entrenched conventions and institutions. Notably, women, in particular, occupied a pivotal role in hosting and participating in these salons, shattering societal constraints and becoming integral to the larger endeavour of fostering a more inclusive and progressive society. Figures of note, such as Madame de Staël, Émilie du Châtelet, and Mary Wollstonecraft, actively championed feminist ideals, vociferously advocating for women's rights, access to education, and the pursuit of social equality. Through their literary compositions and active participation in these intellectual gatherings, these women defied conventional gender norms, contributing significantly to the broader mission of cultivating a more inclusive and progressive society. Moreover, the scientific revolution that unfurled during the Enlightenment epoch constituted a seminal contribution to intellectual resistance. Visionaries such as Isaac Newton, Galileo Galilei, and René Descartes assailed long-cherished beliefs about the natural world, effectively paving the way for a new era of scientific inquiry and rational thought. Newton's groundbreaking principles of motion and universal gravitation, Galileo's audacious heliocentric model of the cosmos, and Descartes' rigorous method of doubt, accompanied by his unwavering commitment to reason, collectively wrought a sea change in the landscape of scientific thought. These advancements engendered a novel worldview that fundamentally challenged established authority and underscored the primacy of empirical evidence as the bedrock of truth. The empowerment of scientific thought dovetailed seamlessly with the overarching objectives of the Enlightenment, fostering an environment wherein individuals felt emboldened to interrogate prevailing paradigms, scrutinise entrenched dogma, and disentangle themselves from oppressive systems. This intellectual rebellion transcended the sphere of politics, permeating the realm of knowledge and heralding an era of profound scientific and philosophical advancement. It is worth noting that the Enlightenment epoch transcended geographical confines, exercising its influence on thinkers and catalysing resistance on a global scale.

In the American context, luminaries such as Thomas Paine and Benjamin Franklin played pivotal roles in shaping the American Revolution, vociferously advocating for independence and the establishment of a democratic republic. Paine's influential pamphlet, "Common Sense," mounted a direct challenge to the authority of the British monarchy, igniting widespread support for American independence. Franklin's scientific experiments, diplomatic endeavours, and prolific literary output underscored the formidable potential of enlightened thinking in pursuing political and social transformation. The ideals of individual rights, liberty, and self-governance germinating during the Enlightenment became foundational principles for the United States and other post-colonial nations, profoundly shaping the trajectory of modern history.

However, it is imperative to recognise that the Enlightenment epoch, despite its lofty ideals of liberty, equality, and reason, was not devoid of flaws and contradictions. While it fervently championed the ideals of the Enlightenment, it frequently marginalised certain segments of society, including women and enslaved individuals, within its discursive ambit and its vision of a more equitable society. Paradoxically, many Enlightenment thinkers, while extolling the virtues of liberty, remained complicit in perpetuating systems of oppression, including but not limited to slavery, colonialism, and gender and racial disparities. These darker facets of the Enlightenment's legacy serve as a stark reminder that intellectual resistance, even when animated by noble ideals, remains susceptible to the biases and limitations inherent to its historical milieu. Recognising these contradictions and the ongoing struggles for comprehensive inclusion and equality remains imperative to our understanding of contemporary societies.

Nevertheless, the intellectual rebellion of the Enlightenment epoch laid a robust foundation for subsequent movements and revolutions, profoundly influencing the course of modern history. The Enlightenment thinkers and litterateurs passionately championed critical thought, the acknowledgement of individual rights, and the relentless pursuit of knowledge as core tenets of democratic societies. Their enduring legacy attests to the transformative potential of ideas and the capacity of individuals to mount a challenge against oppressive systems through intellectual discourse, thereby reshaping prevailing norms and advocating for meaningful social and political change. This legacy finds expression in the development of democratic governance, the advancement of human rights, and the ongoing quest for knowledge and scientific progress, all of which continue to delineate the contours of contemporary society.

# XIXth Century: The Age of Revolutions and Nationalism

The 19th century marks a transformative epoch characterised by a significant shift in societal dynamics and the rise of revolutionary ideologies. Commencing with the unfurling of the French Revolution in 1789, Europe bore witness to a seismic transformation that would indelibly shape the course of history for decades to come. Spanning over a decade, the French Revolution encapsulated a tumultuous era that not only dismantled an age-old monarchy but also gave birth to enduring principles of liberty, equality, and fraternity, resonating deeply with individuals across the globe. This revolution was propelled by profound discontent among the French populace, who shouldered the burdens of feudalism, economic disparities, and political oppression. As the monarchy crumbled, so did the conventional social order, ushering in a new era of revolutionary ideals.

The French Revolution reverberated far beyond France's borders, inciting individuals and communities throughout Europe to challenge oppressive regimes and wholeheartedly embrace the concept of self-determination. Its principles and rallying cries, including "liberty, equality, fraternity," echoed across the continent, offering solace and inspiration to those yearning for autonomy from despotic rule. These echoes of the French Revolution transcended national boundaries, igniting fervent nationalist movements that sought emancipation from colonial powers and attaining national sovereignty. Across Europe, nations such as Greece, Belgium, and Poland passionately fought for independence against imperial forces. In the Americas, Latin American nations rose in defiance against Spanish and Portuguese colonisers, setting in motion a wave of decolonisation.

Nationalism emerged as a dominant force in the 19th century, leaving an indelible mark on political and cultural landscapes. The sense of belonging to a specific nation, steeped in shared history, traditions, and language, served as a unifying element for people striving to assert their identity against external influences. During this period, music, literature, and art emerged as potent expressions of nationalism, reflecting a people's distinctive cultural heritage and fostering a collective sense of pride and belonging. The ascendancy of nationalism generated debates concerning the demarcation of national boundaries and the nature of political allegiance. Some championed ethnically homogeneous nation-states, advocating for the self-determination of distinct cultural groups.

In contrast, others embraced more inclusive notions of civic nationalism, wherein the bond among citizens transcended ethnicity. These debates and conflicts over national identity would continue to shape political discourse for years. Beyond the political and social manifestations of nationalism, the 19th century bore witness to the emergence of potent ideological movements, each offering alternative blueprints for societal transformation. Liberalism, upheld by luminaries like John Stuart Mill and Alexis de Tocqueville, extolled individual rights, limited government intervention, and the pursuit of personal freedom. Socialism, born of mounting inequality and working-class exploitation, clamoured for economic equity and wealth redistribution. Simultaneously, the radical ideology of communism, embodied by Karl Marx and Friedrich Engels, advocated for the abolition of private property and the establishment of a classless society. Resistance against oppressive regimes during this epoch assumed multifarious forms. While armed uprisings, such as the European Revolutions of 1848, manifested in certain regions, political protests, intellectual discourse, and dissemination of revolutionary ideas through publications and secret societies exerted an equivalent influence.

Subterranean networks, like the Carbonari in Italy and the Young Europe movement, endeavoured to coordinate revolutionary activities and foster solidarity among like-minded souls. The impact of the Age of Revolutions and nationalism in the 19th century proved profoundly transformative, fundamentally altering the trajectory of history. The principles and aspirations that emanated from these movements laid the groundwork for developing modern democracies and challenged entrenched power structures. Additionally, these revolutionary fervours redrew borders, dismantled colonialism, and ushered in the birth of new nations.

The 19th century stands as an enduring testament to the indomitable spirit of humanity and its unwavering quest for freedom, justice, and equality. The legacies of the Age of Revolutions and nationalism persist, continuing to shape the contemporary world, reminding us of the potency of resistance, and inspiring us to strive for a more equitable and just society. As we navigate the complexities of the modern era, we must contemplate past lessons and forge a future that upholds the ideals of liberty, equality, and fraternity for all.

# Colonial Resistances: The Struggle for Identity and Autonomy

The era of colonialism bore witness to a myriad of resistance movements across the globe as oppressed populations waged formidable battles against the imposition of foreign dominion and the denial of their inherent rights. These movements stemmed from an ardent yearning for self-determination, preserving cultural identities, and the unwavering pursuit of autonomy.

In Africa, Asia, and the Americas, indigenous peoples and enslaved populations confronted European powers and their colonial apparatuses with unyielding mettle and determination. They resolutely opposed the exploitative practices of colonisers. They ardently fought for their independence while striving to safeguard their cultural heritage and reclaim their sense of self.

These resistance movements manifested in diverse forms, spanning from armed insurrections to peaceful protests and nonviolent acts of defiance, each reflective of the distinct circumstances and aspirations of the communities involved. One notable instance of colonial resistance was witnessed during the American Revolution, where the thirteen colonies mounted a challenge to British rule and ardently pursued sovereignty. Galvanised by Enlightenment ideals and the concept of individual liberty, the trailblazers of this revolution engaged in a relentless struggle to forge a new nation unburdened by the yoke of colonial dominion. Through acts of defiance, such as the Boston Tea Party and the signing of the Declaration of Independence, the American Revolution established a precedent for other movements against colonial powers, serving as an inspirational wellspring and a poignant testament to the possibility of resisting oppression.

In India, the indomitable Mahatma Gandhi emerged as a seminal figure in the battle for independence from British rule. Employing nonviolent resistance, civil disobedience, and peaceful acts of protest, Gandhi and his adherents sought to preserve their cultural identity and secure autonomy for their nation. The Indian independence movement, with its iconic Salt March and the Quit India Movement, assumed the mantle of hope and resilience, influencing other anti-colonial movements on a global scale. Gandhi's principles of nonviolence and his emphasis on the spiritual and moral facets of resistance served as a wellspring of inspiration for generations of activists worldwide.

Africa also bore witness to a multitude of decolonisation movements as nations across the continent waged fervent battles for their emancipation. Leaders such as Kwame Nkrumah in Ghana, Jomo Kenyatta in Kenya, Amílcar Cabral in Guinea-Bissau and Cape Verde, Patrice Lumumba in Congo, and Nelson Mandela in South Africa fervently championed the liberation and self-determination of their people. These leaders galvanised their communities to oppose the oppressive policies of colonial powers. They vociferously advocated for the restoration of their cultural and political autonomy. They envisioned Africa not merely as an independent nation but also as a united continent, nurturing the spirit of Pan-Africanism and championing African unity in the face of persistent exploitation and marginalisation.

In the Americas, resistance against European colonialism assumed diverse forms as well. Indigenous populations in Canada, the United States, and Latin America valiantly resisted land dispossession, forced assimilation, and cultural obliteration. From the resilient struggles of the Apache, Cherokee, and Sioux in the United States to the enduring efforts of the Mapuche in Chile and the Aymara in Bolivia, indigenous communities grappled with formidable challenges in their quest to safeguard their lands and ways of life. The indigenous rights movements in these regions fervently sought recognition of their rights, the preservation of their cultural heritage, and the protection of their ancestral lands. The activism of indigenous leaders such as Eddie Mabo in Australia, Rigoberta Menchu in Guatemala, and Wilma Mankiller in the United States played an instrumental role in raising awareness about the ongoing injustices faced by indigenous peoples and fostering global solidarity.

Colonial resistance extended beyond physical confrontations; it encompassed intellectual and cultural movements. Writers, artists, and intellectuals were pivotal in nurturing a sense of identity and a fervent desire for autonomy among colonised populations. Through their literary and artistic expressions, they contested the dominant colonial narratives. They celebrated the rich cultural heritage and history of their people. These cultural and intellectual contributions emerged as potent forms of resistance, offering alternative perspectives and narratives that countered the dehumanising portrayal of colonised populations.

Several influential writers emerged during this epoch of colonial resistance, significantly contributing to the anti-colonial discourse. Frantz Fanon, an Afro-Caribbean psychiatrist and philosopher, delved into the psychological ramifications of colonialism in his seminal work "The Wretched of the Earth." He contended that the struggle for national liberation and cultural identity necessitated not only political resistance but also a profound process of psychological decolonisation. Fanon's writings called for a radical reevaluation of social, political, and cultural constructs, urging individuals to reclaim their agency and challenge the internalised oppression imposed by colonial powers. His works continue to inspire activists and intellectuals across the globe.Similarly, Aimé Césaire, a Martinican poet and politician, in his groundbreaking work "Discourse on Colonialism," offered a critique of colonialism as a system rife with violence and dehumanisation.

Césaire spotlighted the perniciousness of colonial ideologies and advocated for the repudiation of Western hegemony. His articulations of resistance and decolonisation resonated deeply within colonised communities, providing a conceptual framework for comprehending how colonisation permeated every facet of existence and the pressing imperative to dismantle colonial structures. Through his political activism and writings, Césaire emerged as a prominent figure in the Négritude movement, which sought to reclaim African and African diasporic cultural identities.

In addition to these intellectual contributions, cultural expressions of resistance, including literature, music, and art, played a pivotal role in asserting cultural identities and nurturing a sense of autonomy. For instance, during the Harlem Renaissance of the 1920s, African-American writers, poets, and musicians celebrated their cultural heritage and confronted prevailing racial hierarchies. Langston Hughes, Zora Neale Hurston, and Duke Ellington embraced their African roots. They showcased the richness of Black culture, laying the groundwork for subsequent generations to pursue cultural affirmation and transcend the constraints imposed by a white-dominated society. Their artistic creations emerged as potent tools for challenging stereotypes and affirming the worth and dignity of African-American experiences, influencing the broader civil rights movements that would unfold in the ensuing decades.

While these resistance movements yielded profound impacts, their struggles did not conclude with the formal cessation of colonial rule. Numerous nations continue to grapple with the enduring legacies of colonialism, endeavouring to reclaim their cultural practices, revitalise their languages, and assert their rights on the global stage. Ongoing initiatives to decolonise education, address historical injustices, and preserve cultural heritage remain pivotal in asserting autonomy and fostering a more equitable world.

In summation, colonial resistances constituted multifaceted struggles for identity and autonomy. These movements galvanised individuals and communities united by an unwavering resolve to reclaim their liberty and assert their entitlement to self-determination. The repercussions of these resistances reverberate across time, shaping the post-colonial world and standing as a testament to the indomitable spirit of humanity. Intellectual and cultural contributions further enriched the anti-colonial discourse, challenging colonial ideologies and nurturing a sense of pride and resilience within colonised populations. These collective endeavours continue to influence the ongoing process of decolonisation and the assertion of cultural identities in the contemporary world. The struggles of the past inform the present, serving as a poignant reminder of the significance of empathy, comprehension, and solidarity as we navigate the complexities of our shared global history.

# THE WORLD WARS: RESISTANCE AGAINST OCCUPIERS AND TYRANTS

The commencement of the World Wars during the 20th century ushered in vast devastation and profound anguish while simultaneously giving birth to a myriad of forms of resistance against both occupiers and despots. This chapter explores the valiant acts of defiance that unfolded during this tumultuous epoch in history. We examine the diverse strategies employed by individuals and collectives in their audacious endeavour to challenge the tyrannical regimes that sought to impose their dominion.

## 1. Resistance in Territories under Occupation:

World War I and II witnessed the occupation of numerous nations by hostile forces. Within these occupied domains emerged resistance movements driven by an unwavering commitment to safeguard national identity, defy military subjugation, and strive toward emancipation. These movements adopted a multifarious array of tactics, spanning from the art of guerrilla warfare and acts of subversion to the establishment of covert networks and the art of intelligence procurement. During the span of World War II, the French Resistance, known as La Résistance, emerged as an emblem of unyielding opposition to Nazi occupation. This resistance effort encompassed a tapestry of diverse groups and individuals comprising both genders. Their endeavours encompassed acts of bombing, targeted assassinations, and acts of sabotage, all while providing indispensable intelligence to the Allied forces. The disruptive impact of their actions on German military operations was profound, bolstering civilian morale and paving the way for the eventual liberation of France.

## 2. The Role of Subterranean Networks:

Subterranean networks played a pivotal role in underpinning resistance endeavours during the epoch of the World Wars. These clandestine networks served as sanctuaries of refuge, hubs for creating counterfeit documentation, conduits for the clandestine transportation of vital supplies, and orchestration centres for acts of subversion. The individuals who undertook these perilous missions risked their existence in the relentless pursuit of intelligence gathering, thus ensuring the success of resistance undertakings. Within the context of World War II, the Zegota organisation epitomised the potency of underground networks. Zegota, signifying the "Council to Aid Jews," engaged in an unwavering mission to effect the rescue of Jewish individuals and provide them with shelter, sustenance, and fabricated identification credentials. Guided by a diverse cadre of activists, intellectuals, and religious leaders, Zegota managed to preserve the lives of thousands of Jewish individuals, a testimony to the remarkable valour and solidarity exhibited even in the face of dire personal risk.

## 3. Partisans and the Art of Guerrilla Warfare:

Partisan collectives and guerrilla combatants clandestinely operated behind enemy lines, orchestrating a series of ambushes, wreaking havoc upon vital infrastructure, and mounting acts of sabotage that disrupted military operations. These champions of resistance exhibited an aptitude for unorthodox stratagems, adroitly adapting to the distinctive challenges presented by their environments and sowing seeds of trepidation within the hearts of the occupying forces. The Yugoslav Partisans, under the stewardship of Josip Broz Tito, waged an unrelenting guerrilla campaign against Axis forces during World War II. Hailing from the remote enclaves of mountains and densely forested regions, the Partisans undertook daring hit-and-run assaults, severing critical supply lines and conscripting fighters from an eclectic spectrum of backgrounds. Their unyielding resistance served to immobilise substantial enemy resources and played a pivotal role in the battle against Nazi occupation within the Balkan territories.

## 4. Rebellions within the Confines of Concentration Camps:

In the face of unfathomable horrors, incarcerated individuals within concentration camps meticulously choreographed acts of insurrection. These acts, ranging from meticulously orchestrated uprisings to isolated manifestations of defiance, were executed to preserve human dignity, inflict harm upon their captors, and kindle flames of hope within an otherwise bleak existence. One particularly salient instance is the Warsaw Ghetto Uprising of 1943. Confronting the spectre of deportation and extermination, the Jewish residents of the Warsaw Ghetto mounted an armed insurrection against the Nazi forces. Despite being overwhelmingly outnumbered and outgunned, these brave fighters tenaciously held their ground for an extended period, inflicting substantial casualties upon the German troops. Their unflinching resistance was a poignant testament to their indomitable resolve to oppose oppression. It served as an inspirational beacon, catalysing subsequent uprisings within other Nazi concentration camps.

## 5. Resistance from Within the Ranks of Occupying Forces:

It is a historical verity that not all individuals serving within occupying forces did so with unswerving compliance to the oppressive regimes they represented. A clandestine cadre of individuals within these occupying forces covertly aligned themselves with the resistance movements, thereby providing invaluable intelligence, engaging in acts of subterfuge, and assisting the local populace. These manifestations of resistance from within the very bosom of the enemy's ranks exerted a transformative influence, ultimately contributing to the erosion of the occupiers' endeavours. Within the precincts of the German military establishment, a diminutive assemblage known as the White Rose emerged as a paragon of valour in their battle against Nazi despotism. Comprising predominantly of university students and their erudite professors, they clandestinely disseminated anti-Nazi missives, imploring their compatriots to defy Hitler's autocratic regime. Notwithstanding the severe reprisals they endured, including the execution of several members, their actions attested to the capacity for resistance to materialise from the most unexpected quarters. Even within the crucible of totalitarianism, these resolute individuals embodied the capacity of a few intrepid souls to challenge the status quo.

## 6. Resistance Against Tyranny:

The World Wars bore witness to resistance movements that arose to challenge tyrants who sought to consolidate their dominion within their nations. These movements took shape as bulwarks against autocratic rule, the propounding of fascist ideologies, and the stifling of civil liberties. In Italy, where the Fascist regime of Benito Mussolini held sway, the Italian Resistance materialised as a formidable adversary to his authoritarian governance. Comprising a diverse panorama of ideological perspectives and political affiliations, the Italian Resistance undertook acts of sabotage, the art of intelligence acquisition, and the execution of guerrilla warfare. Their actions were instrumental in weakening Mussolini's stranglehold on power, thereby contributing to the eventual liberation of Italy by the Allied forces.

## 7. Civil Disobedience and the Art of Nonviolent Resistance:

Not all expressions of resistance during the World Wars manifested in armed confrontations. Civil disobedience and the art of nonviolent resistance emerged as influential modalities for challenging oppressive regimes. From strikes and protest demonstrations to clandestine publications and subversive literary endeavours, these expressions of resistance sought to erode the authority and legitimacy of tyrannical regimes. In the context of British colonial rule in India, Mahatma Gandhi harnessed the power of nonviolent resistance to contest the dominion of the British colonial apparatus and fervently advocated for Indian independence. Through acts of civil disobedience, such as the Salt March and the Quit India Movement, Gandhi laid bare the oppressive nature of colonial rule and galvanised millions to join the struggle for emancipation. His modus operandi of nonviolence became an omnipotent instrument for resistance movements worldwide.

## 8. The Integral Role of Women in the Tapestry of Resistance:

The active participation of women inexorably enriched the panorama of resistance movements during the World Wars. From their engagement in espionage and service as couriers to their vital contributions to intelligence acquisition and the nursing of wounded combatants, women made a resounding impact, showcasing their mettle and courage in the face of adversity. Their contributions were indubitably pivotal in determining the outcomes of numerous resistance operations. Within the precincts of the Soviet Union, an untold multitude of women rallied to the banner of the partisan struggle, fighting shoulder-to-shoulder with their male counterparts against the encroaching tide of German invaders. The Night Witches, an exclusively female aviation regiment, executed daring nocturnal bombing sorties that sowed terror within the hearts of their adversaries. The feats of individuals such as Lyudmila Pavlichenko, a sniper whose tally of confirmed kills numbered an astounding 309, and Zoya Kosmodemyanskaya, an iconic martyr of the Soviet partisan movement, bore testimony to the profound impact of women within the tapestry of resistance.

## In Closing:

The World Wars were epochs marked by profound human suffering. However, they also witnessed extraordinary acts of resistance against occupiers and tyrants. From the clandestine networks and guerrilla warfare to the art of nonviolent resistance and the indomitable contributions of women, resistance emerged as an indomitable force that left an indelible imprint upon the course of global conflicts. The valour and sacrifices of those who resisted serve as a resounding testament to the unquenchable spirit of humanity when faced with the spectre of oppression.

# THE COLD WAR AND BEYOND: IDEOLOGICAL RESISTANCES

The Cold War era, from the end of World War II to the early 1990s, was a period of significant global tension between two superpowers: the United States and the Soviet Union. This era was characterised by ideological conflict as nations, groups, and individuals opposed the dominant ideologies of communism and capitalism.

One of the prominent forms of ideological opposition during the Cold War was anti-communism, which manifested in various ways. In the United States, for instance, the government launched an extensive campaign known as the Red Scare, targeting individuals suspected of communist sympathies. This resulted in the persecution and blacklisting of many writers, actors, and artists considered subversive or a threat to American values during the McCarthyism.

The anti-communist sentiment in the United States was fueled by apprehension and anxiety over the spread of communism, especially following the communist victory in China in 1949 and the onset of the

Korean War in 1950. In response, the US government implemented aggressive measures to root out suspected communist influence. The House Un-American Activities Committee (HUAC) initiated investigations into alleged communist activities, subjecting individuals to interrogations and compelling them to testify against their colleagues. This atmosphere of fear and suspicion had a chilling effect on freedom of expression and stifled dissent. It was a time in American history that saw US Sen. Joseph McCarthy of Wisconsin produce a series of investigations and hearings during the 1950s to expose supposed communist infiltration of various areas of the US government. The term "McCarthyism" is now used more broadly to describe any reckless, unsubstantiated accusations or defamation of character or reputation through such tactics.

Similarly, within the Soviet Union and its satellite states, dissidents emerged as a potent force of ideological resistance. These individuals, often called dissident writers, artists, and intellectuals, challenged the communist regime's authoritarianism through their creative works. They utilised literature, art, and underground publications to express their dissent and reveal the realities of their life in the Soviet bloc.

One notable figure in this movement was Alexander Solzhenitsyn, a renowned Russian writer and Nobel Laureate. Solzhenitsyn's works, including "One Day in the Life of Ivan Denisovich" and "The Gulag Archipelago," exposed the Soviet Gulag system (much resembling the US Guantanamo detention camp established by Bush after the invasion of Afghanistan). The repression faced by ordinary citizens under the communist regime exposed in Solzhenitsyn's writings has been inflated by the Western propaganda machine to demonise communism, socialism, and, in this context, any third-world liberation ideology that opposed the Western capitalist hegemony.

In the Arab world, for example, Nasserism, Baathism, socialism and Pan-Arab nationalism were considered enemy ideologies. As all of them are secularist, the West, led by the USA, worked with ultra-conservative Arab governments and, together, funded and empowered Islamist groups and networks to fight Nasser, the Baathists, and the socialists, with all means, terrorism included. Thus, they supported and primarily produced or contributed to creating and empowering - undercover – the major brands of what they called later on "terrorists". After using them against the Soviet troops in Afghanistan, the former "Islamist" militants became uncontrollable to the degree that Usama ben Laden proposed to "liberate" Saudi Arabia, a close US- ally at the time. Al-Sahwa was dubbed "terrorism", and the "Mujahedeen" (or the valuable fools) who served the US global strategy to "free" Afghanistan from the Red Army grew so dangerous that Washington put over two decennies to expel them from their Afghan base (Al-Qaeda, in Arabic, means base). But the price was extremely high for Americans who paid it on 9 September 2001.

In addition to individual acts of resistance, the Cold War witnessed more significant ideological resistances, such as decolonisation movements in former colonies. Across Asia, Africa, and Latin America, many nations fought against their colonial oppressors, seeking independence and self-determination. These movements were often motivated by ideological principles, as colonised populations sought to free themselves from the dominance of Western capitalist powers.

Frantz Fanon, a psychiatrist and writer from Martinique, played a notable role in the decolonisation movement. His seminal work, "The Wretched of the Earth," eloquently depicted colonisation's psychological and physical effects on the colonised. Fanon argued that true liberation from colonial oppression required a complete rejection of the coloniser's culture and values. His ideas profoundly influenced liberation movements worldwide, inspiring activists to embrace revolutionary violence to overthrow their oppressors.

Furthermore, the Cold War era also witnessed the rise of countercultural movements that rebelled against mainstream ideologies. The 1960s and 1970s saw protest movements advocating for civil rights, gender equality, and opposition to war. These movements, often fueled by values of freedom, peace, and social justice, aimed to challenge prevailing power structures and establish alternative systems based on equality and justice.

In the United States, the Civil Rights Movement, led by influential figures like Martin Luther King Jr. and Malcolm X, sought to dismantle systemic racism and achieve equal rights for African Americans. Their nonviolent protests and powerful speeches galvanised the nation and forced it to confront deep-seated prejudices. Similarly, the feminist movement, led by prominent figures such as Gloria Steinem and Betty Friedan, challenged gender norms and fought for women's rights, leading to significant societal shifts in attitudes toward gender equality.

As the Cold War drew close, ideological resistance continued to shape the world. The collapse of the Soviet Union, which was to some extent the undercover work of the CIA, created a vacuum that was quickly occupied by radical Islamist opposition movements, both locally (in Arab and Muslim-majority countries) and globally: it was the rise of the Islamist wave called by some Saudi theoreticians, the Wake-Up (Al-Sahwa). On the other hand, Non-governmental organisations (NGOs) and human rights activists emerged as crucial advocates for social justice, democracy, and freedom of expression.

The post-Cold War era strengthened transnational movements as activists addressed global issues such as climate change, poverty, and corporate power. For instance, the anti-globalisation movement critiqued neoliberal capitalism's impacts and called for more equitable economic systems. The World Social Forum, a gathering of activists and organisations worldwide, provided a platform for exchanging ideas and strategies to challenge dominant economic and political structures.

Technological advancements, particularly the rise of the internet and social media, further facilitated ideological resistance. Digital platforms offered new avenues for dissent, enabling individuals and groups to mobilise, share ideas, and challenge dominant narratives. Movements like the Arab Spring and Occupy Wall Street demonstrated the power of digital resistance in mobilising populations and demanding change.

The Arab Spring, a series of uprisings across the Middle East and North Africa, was primarily driven by social media platforms like Facebook and Twitter. These platforms allowed individuals to organise protests, disseminate information, and rally support for their cause. The self-immolation of Tunisian street vendor Mohamed Bouazizi, in protest of government oppression, symbolised resistance and inspired a wave of uprisings in the region.

Similarly, the Occupy Wall Street movement began in 2011 and used social media to amplify voices protesting economic inequality and corporate influence in politics. The movement's critique of the "1%" and calls for economic justice resonated globally, leading to similar actions in other countries.

The Cold War and its aftermath represent critical periods of ideological resistance. They shaped the political, cultural, and social landscapes of nations worldwide. Ideological opposition during this time was not confined to a single ideology or geographic location but rather a complex tapestry of interconnected movements and individuals challenging the status quo and striving for a more just and equitable world.

The Cold War era also witnessed forms of ideological resistance beyond politics and social justice. Artists and intellectuals played a vital role in challenging dominant cultural and artistic norms, pushing the boundaries of creativity and self-expression. The avant-garde movement emerged as a force of resistance against traditional artistic conventions, seeking to disrupt established norms and explore new artistic possibilities.

Artists such as Pablo Picasso, Salvador Dali, and Jackson Pollock embraced unconventional forms, abstract expressionism, and surrealism to create works that challenged traditional notions of beauty and representation. Their art often mirrored the Cold War era's chaos and uncertainty, reflecting the time's anxieties and contradictions.

Picasso's famous painting, "Guernica," is a powerful testament to the horrors of war and the suffering inflicted on innocent civilians. Created in response to the bombing of the town of Guernica during the Spanish Civil War, the painting depicts the brutality and destruction of war, capturing the pain and anguish of the victims. "Guernica" became a symbol of anti-war sentiment and a powerful tool for resistance against the violence and aggression of the time.

Similarly, in literature, writers like Samuel Beckett and Albert Camus challenged conventional narrative structures and explored existential themes. Beckett's play, "Waiting for Godot," embodies the absurdity of human existence and the futility of waiting for salvation or meaning in a chaotic world. On the other hand, Camus explored the themes of existentialism and the search for meaning in his novel, "The Stranger." These literary works defied the conventions of storytelling and questioned the foundations of human existence, resisting the prevailing ideologies of the Cold War era.

Beyond art and culture, religion and spirituality were also arenas of ideological resistance during the Cold War era. Religious leaders and movements played vital roles in advocating for peace, justice, and human rights, challenging the dominant narratives of the superpowers.

One example is the Civil Rights Movement in the United States, where prominent figures like Martin Luther King Jr. and other religious leaders utilised the power of faith and moral principles to advocate for racial equality. Their resistance against racial discrimination was grounded in the belief in the inherent dignity and worth of every individual, regardless of their race or background.

Similarly, in Latin America, the Liberation Theology movement emerged as a strong force of resistance against social and economic inequalities. Influenced by Marxist ideas and the teachings of Jesus, Liberation Theology sought to address poverty, injustice, and oppression, advocating for the rights of the poor and marginalised. Figures like Archbishop Oscar Romero of El Salvador became iconic symbols of resistance and solidarity.

The Cold War era and ideological tensions created fertile ground for resistance in various forms and arenas. Behind the veil of politics and global power struggles, individuals, writers, artists, religious leaders, and activists all found ways to challenge the dominant ideologies and strive for a more just and equitable world.

While the specific contexts and forms of resistance have evolved since the end of the Cold War, the spirit of ideological resistance continues to shape our world today. The fight against injustice, inequality, and oppression remains as relevant now as it was during the Cold War era. From grassroots movements advocating for climate justice to activists calling for racial equality and gender liberation, the legacy of ideological resistance is alive and thriving.

The Cold War era serves as a reminder of the power of ideas and the transformative potential of resistance. It reminds us that in the face of dominant ideologies and oppressive systems, individuals and communities can challenge the status quo and work towards a more inclusive and just society.

As the world continues to grapple with new challenges and ideologies, it is crucial to draw inspiration from the history of ideological resistance and learn from the strategies and tactics employed by those who came before us. By studying the movements, individuals, and ideas that resisted the dominant ideologies of the Cold War era, we can gain insight into the power of collective action, the importance of solidarity, and the necessity of challenging unjust systems.

The legacy of ideological resistance during the Cold War era calls on us to remain vigilant, to question prevailing narratives, and to challenge oppressive systems wherever they exist. It serves as a reminder that change is possible and that pursuing a more just and equitable world is a continuous struggle that requires ongoing resistance, resilience, and imagination.

# Modern Era: Digital Revolutions and The Power of Information

In the contemporary era, we have witnessed an unparalleled transformation in the manifestation of resistance. The advent of the digital age, coupled with the ascent of the internet and mass communication technologies, has revolutionised how individuals organise and articulate their dissent.

The potency of information has wrought a metamorphosis upon the terrain of resistance movements, reconfiguring the dynamics of activism and confronting established power structures. With a click of a button, individuals can now disseminate their ideas globally, reaching audiences hitherto inconceivable. This newfound accessibility has democratised resistance, amplifying marginalised voices and catalysing a fresh wave of grassroots movements.

Social media platforms have evolved into formidable instruments for mobilising kindred spirits, orchestrating coordinated actions, and raising awareness regarding injustices transcending borders. The ease with which information, images, and videos can be shared online has proven instrumental in drawing attention to systemic issues and facilitating collective action. Noteworthy examples include hashtags like #BlackLivesMatter, #MeToo, and #FridaysForFuture, which have ignited international dialogues, galvanised support, and pressured institutions to address systemic problems.

One of the most conspicuous instances of this modern-day resistance is the Arab Spring, a series of uprisings that swept through the Middle East and North Africa in 2011. Protesters harnessed the power of social media platforms such as Twitter and Facebook to orchestrate demonstrations, disseminate real-time information, and expose government corruption. This unprecedented technology deployment enabled the rapid dissemination of information, dismantling traditional communication barriers and challenging entrenched power structures.

Furthermore, the repercussions of the digital revolution extend beyond social movements. It has fundamentally reshaped how individuals seek and consume information. Historically, sources of news and information were subject to the control of a select few gatekeepers, such as newspapers, television networks, and publishing houses. However, the ascent of the internet has democratised access to information, ushering in a wide spectrum of sources and perspectives. This democratisation of information has had profound ramifications for resistance movements.

Activists can now access alternative news sources, grassroots blogs, and independent journalism, all offering nuanced perspectives often absent in mainstream media. Consequently, resistance movements have become better informed and interconnected, fostering a deeper comprehension of the issues and a more robust capacity to challenge prevailing narratives.

Furthermore, the internet has facilitated the formation of virtual communities characterised by shared interests and objectives. Online platforms enable individuals to forge connections and collaborate with like-minded individuals, creating global networks of solidarity. These digital communities provide emotional support, share resources, and amplify each other's messages, cultivating a sense of belonging and empowering individuals to take decisive action. The capacity to access information effortlessly and instantaneously has also empowered citizens to hold governments and institutions accountable.

Whistleblowers, exemplified by figures such as Edward Snowden, have harnessed the internet as a tool to expose covert surveillance programs and infringements on privacy perpetrated by intelligence agencies. The release of classified documents initiated a global discourse on the balance between security and individual rights, ultimately leading to reforms and enhanced transparency in certain nations. Moreover, the digital age has engendered novel forms of resistance, including hacktivism and cyber warfare. These unconventional tactics involve using computer technology to disrupt or unveil systems and networks perpetuating injustice. From activist hackers targeting oppressive regimes to state-sanctioned cyberattacks, the digital sphere has transformed into a battleground for ideological confrontations and power dynamics. However, it is imperative to acknowledge that the digital age presents challenges. While the internet has opened up new avenues for resistance, it has simultaneously introduced fresh obstacles. Governments and corporations have employed surveillance technologies to monitor and regulate online activities, curtailing dissent and infringing privacy. The dissemination of counterfeit news and disinformation campaigns has also eroded the credibility of online information, rendering it increasingly arduous to distinguish veracity from manipulation.

In this contemporary era, resistance transcends the confines of physical protests, demonstrations, or offline activism alone. The influence of information and the digital revolution has ushered new prospects for individuals and groups to challenge authority, foster societal transformation, and shape public opinion. The digital realm has become integral to contemporary resistance, facilitating global connections, amplifying voices, and mobilising efforts to pursue a more just and equitable world.

As we navigate this ever-evolving digital landscape, we must subject our actions to rigorous scrutiny, ensuring our resistance remains anchored in the relentless pursuit of justice, truth, and freedom. The power of information, while transformative, necessitates responsible utilisation, ethical considerations, and an unwavering commitment to nurturing inclusive and diverse online spaces. By harnessing the potential of the digital age, we can continue to push the boundaries of resistance, challenge oppressive systems, and forge a brighter future for all.

# Resistance in Arts and Culture

Art has always been an unwavering bastion, steadfastly standing as a powerful medium for expressing dissent, a platform for challenging the prevailing status quo, and a source of profound inspiration for resistance. Its enduring relevance resonates across the annals of history, where artists and cultural luminaries have harnessed their creative talents to illuminate the shadows of social injustice, dissect the intricacies of political inequities, and lay bare the stark realities of economic disparities. In doing so, they have catalysed introspection, nurtured spirited discourse, and, above all, ignited the flames of change and transformation.

Within the framework of this discourse, we delve ever deeper into the labyrinthine nuances of the role of resistance in the realm of arts and culture, seeking to not only spotlight but also unravel the manifold forms and mediums through which artists, visionaries, and creatives alike have waged valiant battles against the spectre of oppression, wielding their pens, brushes, voices, and imaginations as potent weapons in the ceaseless struggle for a fairer, more equitable world.

The empire of visual arts stands as a citadel of resistance, where creative minds have wielded the mighty brushstroke and the evocative image as formidable weapons in their arsenal. From the biting satire of political cartoons that pierce through the armour of oppressive systems to the covert acts of graffiti artists who dare to scrawl messages of dissent on the walls of conformity, visual artists have fearlessly embraced the canvas as a battleground of ideas. Iconic works such as Pablo Picasso's haunting "Guernica" serve as unforgettable testimonies to the horrors of war, the unrelenting suffering of civilians, and the collective resolve to resist the looming spectre of fascism. Nevertheless, the power of resistance extends beyond the realm of the visible, as the lens of photography has also been harnessed to chronicle pivotal moments, document the fervour of protests, and expose the raw nerve of injustices to the gaze of the world. The indomitable image of the lone "Tank Man" standing defiantly before a column of armoured vehicles during the tumultuous Tiananmen Square protests of 1989 stands as an enduring symbol of resistance against the iron fist of authoritarianism.

However, the canvas of resistance in the visual arts extends far beyond explicit political statements.

Symbolism and metaphors have, time and again, been employed as nuanced forms of resistance, where artists such as Frida Kahlo and Diego Rivera have deftly wielded surrealist techniques and vivid symbolism to raise consciousness regarding personal struggles, the gross abuses of human rights, and the harrowing plight of indigenous communities. This approach transcends the boundaries of mere political commentary, allowing their art to become a universal language that speaks to the hearts and minds of individuals from diverse backgrounds, transcending the boundaries of nations and cultures.

Literature, too, unfurls as a rich tapestry interwoven with threads of resistance.

Renowned authors such as George Orwell, through masterpieces like "1984," have skillfully employed the medium of fiction to serve as cautionary tales, sounding the alarm against the perils of totalitarianism and championing the primacy of individual freedom. By conjuring vivid and often dystopian visions of the future, these literary luminaries have offered readers a stark mirror to examine the potential consequences of unchecked power, serving as beacons of vigilance against the creeping shadows of authoritarianism. Similarly, authors such as Chinua Achebe, Arundhati Roy, and Toni Morrison have lent their pens and voices to amplify the narratives of marginalised communities, shining an unrelenting spotlight on issues ranging from colonialism and racism to gender inequality. Their eloquent prose and unflinching narratives have acted as catalysts for social change, urging readers to question the established norms, challenge the existing paradigms, and take up the mantle of justice.

In music, the harmony of resistance has often served as a powerful unifying force in times of tumultuous change. Protest songs have emerged as anthems for movements, their lyrics carrying the collective hopes, aspirations, and demands of a generation seeking justice and equality. From the heartland of the civil rights movement in the United States, where anthems like "We Shall Overcome" echoed through the streets, to the distant shores of South Africa, where iconic figures like Miriam Makeba and Hugh Masekela used their music as a call to action in the fight against apartheid, melodies have become the beating heart of social transformation. Genres like hip-hop, reggae, and folk music have transcended the boundaries of entertainment, serving as platforms for marginalised communities to articulate their grievances, voice their aspirations, and demand a reckoning with the entrenched systems of injustice.

Performance arts, too, have etched their mark on the canvas of resistance, providing a hallowed stage for the voices of the marginalised to reverberate with unyielding clarity. Theatre, dance, and performance art have served as crucibles for questioning societal norms, the scrutiny of authority, and the exposure of the fault lines within oppressive systems. The works of pioneering playwrights such as Bertolt Brecht and Augusto Boal have embraced techniques such as epic theatre and forum theatre to engage audiences on a visceral level, prodding them to question the status quo and interrogate the social and political structures they often take for granted. For instance, Brecht's concept of alienation sought to dismantle the illusion of realism in theatre, compelling audiences to cast a critical eye on the constructs of their societies.

In the digital age, resistance within arts and culture has adopted new forms, seizing the potential of social media platforms, podcasts, and online art exhibitions as arenas for creative expression and societal transformation. Online movements such as #BlackLivesMatter and #MeToo have witnessed the extraordinary power of digital spaces, where voices once silenced or marginalised find resonance, organising protests and catalysing change. Moreover, the frontiers of virtual and augmented reality technologies have continued to expand, providing artists with innovative tools for immersive storytelling. These technologies enable artists to craft experiences that immerse audiences in the stark realities of oppressed communities, fostering empathy and motivating action.

Artists and cultural icons have persistently occupied the vanguard of resistance movements. Their unwavering courage, boundless creativity, and unyielding determination to confront the established order have inspired generations and initiated conversations that have steered influential social and political metamorphoses. Through the tapestry of their artistry, they have underscored a profound truth: that resistance extends beyond the realm of physical confrontation and is manifest through the boundless realms of imagination, creativity, and the art of storytelling. However, the path of resistance within arts and culture has challenges and tribulations. Artists often find themselves pitted against the forces of censorship, repression, and even violence as the consequences of their bold expressions. Governments and authorities, keen on preserving their dominion, may seek to stifle dissenting voices, viewing art as a potent threat to their hegemony. Throughout history, numerous artists have faced persecution, imprisonment, or been compelled into exile due to the audacity of their defiant works. However, they continue to inspire others to resist, rise against the tide, and champion justice through their resilience and steadfast commitment to their artistic vision.

Furthermore, resistance within arts and culture does not always receive unanimous acclaim. Certain works may ignite controversy, provoke criticism, and even incite backlash from those at odds with the conveyed messages. Artists grapple with navigating the turbulent waters of societal divisions, addressing multifaceted issues, and striking a delicate balance between stirring thought and potentially alienating audiences. Paradoxically, these contentious works often lead to the most profound dialogues and the most transformative conversations and compel society to confront uncomfortable truths. For resistance within arts and culture to truly take root and wield its full transformative potential, it necessitates the active engagement of audiences. Through dialogue, introspection, and decisive action, the seeds of resistance sown by artists can flourish into tangible change. Audiences are beckoned not merely to consume passively but to actively listen, participate, question, and remain open to the challenges posed by the established norms. In doing so, they become indispensable allies in the resistance movement, amplifying the voices of artists and ushering in a more just, equitable, and enlightened society.

In summation, resistance within the arts and culture emerges as a formidable and enduring force that transcends epochs. Artists, visionaries, and creatives, driven by an unwavering commitment to challenging oppressive systems, kindling change, and providing a resounding voice for the marginalised, continue to employ their talents as a catalyst for conversation, a force for disrupting established narratives, and a beacon of hope that ignites the enthusiasm of resistance. By scrutinising the multifaceted tapestry of resistance within the arts, we understand how creativity can serve as a potent instrument for change in the world. This exploration of resistance within the arts and culture is an enduring testament to the indomitable power of human expression and the relentless pursuit of justice and equity.

# The Philosophy of Resistance in the XXIst Century

In the 21st century, the concept of resistance has undergone a significant evolution, encompassing a diverse range of philosophical perspectives and methodologies. It extends far beyond its traditional boundaries, now encompassing intellectual, social, and cultural dimensions alongside physical acts of defiance. This chapter focuses on the landscape of resistance philosophy, offering insights into its response to the intricate challenges posed by the modern world.

One prominent philosophy of resistance in the 21st century is post-structuralism, championed by eminent thinkers such as Michel Foucault and Judith Butler. These scholars have fearlessly challenged conventional power structures and ideologies, emphasising the imperative to resist dominant discourses perpetuating inequality and oppression. According to them, resistance involves unveiling and deconstructing the concealed power dynamics that quietly shape our existence.

Foucault's influential concept of power-knowledge underscores the interplay between power and knowledge production within society. He posits that power is not merely imposed upon individuals but intricately woven into social institutions and practices. Consequently, resistance necessitates a profound examination and subversion of these structures of power knowledge, challenging established norms and revealing covert mechanisms of control. Foucault also delves into the notion of counter-conduct, which involves subversive acts and tactics capable of disrupting and challenging the normalising power of institutions. Through counter-conduct, individuals can resist and construct alternative modes of existence.

Butler's groundbreaking concept of gender performativity expands the realm of resistance, mainly concerning matters of sexuality and gender identity. She posits that gender is not an inherent category but rather a social construct performed by individuals. In this context, resistance involves disrupting and defying normative gender roles, affirming the validity of diverse gender identities. By refusing to conform to societal expectations, individuals disrupt the power dynamics that uphold oppressive gender norms. Furthermore, Butler underscores the importance of collective action and solidarity within resistance movements, emphasising that marginalised groups can draw strength and support from collective resistance against oppressive structures.

Another significant philosophical perspective in the realm of resistance is existentialism. Existentialist philosophers like Jean-Paul Sartre and Albert Camus underscore the importance of individual freedom and authenticity as the foundation of resistance. They contend that resisting societal pressures and expectations necessitates individuals embracing their autonomy and taking responsibility for their actions.

Sartre's concept of radical freedom posits that individuals are not mere products of external circumstances but possess the power to transcend them through their choices. According to Sartre, resistance entails asserting one's freedom and actively engaging in actions aligned with one's values and beliefs. By claiming their subjectivity, individuals resist being reduced to objects or products of their circumstances. Sartre also delves into the ethics and responsibility associated with resistance, highlighting the importance of considering the impact of one's actions on others and society as a whole.

On the other hand, Camus delves into the philosophical exploration of the absurd in a seemingly chaotic and irrational world. He argues that individuals must confront the absurdity of existence and actively rebel against it. This rebellion involves rejecting meaninglessness and striving for personal integrity and authenticity within a universe devoid of inherent purpose. Camus introduces the concept of the rebel, an individual who resists in the face of adversity and refuses to accept the absurd as the ultimate truth. The rebel's resistance is not necessarily aimed at achieving a specific goal. However, it serves as an affirmation of human dignity and a defiance against absurdity.

Moreover, the philosophy of resistance in the 21st century extends its reach to encompass environmentalism and ecological resistance. With the growing awareness of climate change and the degradation of natural habitats, many philosophers argue that resistance must now encompass the protection of our planet. Environmental activists, inspired by thinkers like Vandana Shiva and Arne Naess, advocate for a profound connection with nature and the imperative to resist human actions that harm the environment.

Shiva's ecofeminist philosophy underscores the intersectionality of environmental and gender-based oppressions. She contends that the exploitation of nature is intrinsically linked to the exploitation of women, both stemming from a patriarchal and capitalist worldview that prioritises profit over the well-being of people and the Earth. In this context, resistance involves forging alternative ways of living that challenge the dominant paradigm, emphasising ecological sustainability and gender equity. Shiva also highlights the significance of traditional ecological knowledge and indigenous wisdom in guiding resistance movements and promoting sustainable practices.

Naess introduces the concept of deep ecology, advocating for a fundamental shift in the human-nature relationship from dominance to deep interconnectedness and respect. Deep ecologists argue that resistance lies in recognising the intrinsic value of all life forms and promoting ecological citizenship. This calls for individuals to actively strive to protect and restore ecological systems through personal and collective action. Naess also emphasises the importance of self-realisation and personal transformation in cultivating a deep ecological consciousness that informs resistance to environmental degradation.

Additionally, the rise of technology and the digital age has given birth to new forms of resistance. Online activism and hacktivism have become potent tools for challenging authority and championing social justice. From the Arab Spring to the Occupy Wall Street movement, social media and digital platforms have played a pivotal role in mobilising resistance and amplifying the voices of marginalised communities.

Activists and thinkers, exemplified by the cyberphilosopher Alexander Galloway, analyse how various forms of power exploit digital networks. They argue that resistance in the digital age necessitates the disruption and subversion of the control exerted by governments and corporations over information flows and online spaces. Hacktivist groups like Anonymous embody this resistance by exposing corruption and advocating for transparency, blurring the boundaries between the virtual and physical realms. Galloway also explores the concept of radical transparency as a form of resistance wherein individuals and organisations challenge the surveillance and control mechanisms of powerful entities.

Furthermore, the 21st century has witnessed the rise of intersectional resistance. This philosophy recognises the interdependence of various forms of oppression and calls for collective action against multiple systems of domination. Intersectional resistance emphasises the importance of addressing issues related to race, gender, class, and other identity axes in creating meaningful and effective resistance movements.

Drawing from the work of scholars like Kimberlé Crenshaw and Bell Hooks, intersectional resistance challenges the tendency to prioritise a single issue or identity over others. It underscores the necessity of recognising and addressing how different forms of oppression intersect and compound one another. By embracing intersectionality, resistance movements can foster solidarity and inclusivity, dismantling the hierarchical structures perpetuating injustice. Crenshaw also explores the concept of intersectional feminism, which centres on the experiences and voices of marginalised women within resistance movements.

Overall, the philosophy of resistance in the 21st century mirrors our world's dynamic and ever-changing nature. It acknowledges that resistance manifests in diverse forms and is not bound by any particular ideology or methodology. As we navigate the complexities of our time, philosophers and activists continually explore fresh avenues for challenging the status quo and advocating for a more just and equitable world. The philosophies discussed in this chapter provide a robust foundation for comprehending and engaging in resistance, whether through intellectual critique, social activism, environmental stewardship, or the use of technology. By integrating these diverse perspectives and embracing intersectionality, individuals and communities can work towards transformative change and liberation from oppressive power systems.

# RESISTANCE IN LITERATURE

Resistance in literature has perennially emerged as a multifaceted and recurring theme, consistently inspiring and intellectually challenging readers throughout the annals of literary history. From the narratives of antiquity to contemporary works of fiction, literature has been an instrumental domain for authors to effectively portray various manifestations of resistance against prevailing structures of oppression, societal norms, and injustices. This chapter examines the profound significance of resistance within the literary sphere, exploring its historical contextualisation, psychological impact on its readers, and profound transformative potential in reflecting and actively shaping societies.

## 1. The Literary Medium as a Vehicle for Resistance:

Throughout epochs, literature has remained a formidable platform that provides writers with the agency to express dissent, challenge established paradigms, and question the status quo. The narrative canvases that authors employ serve as illuminating portals into the ordeals confronted by marginalised individuals and communities, effectively fostering empathy and engendering a heightened social consciousness amongst its readership. By juxtaposing alternative perspectives and subjecting existing power structures to critical scrutiny, literature effectively equips individuals to question prevailing norms and articulate their voices when confronting adversities. Throughout history, literary creations have emerged as instrumental agents of transformative change, serving as catalysts for catalysing discourse, shaping public opinion, and galvanising movements that seek to usher in social reform.

## 2. Artistic Portrayal of Individual Acts of Resistance:

One of the captivating attributes of literature is its ability to vividly depict the unwavering tenacity displayed by individuals who defy societal expectations and challenge established norms. These literary figures stand as luminous exemplars of courage and determination, beckoning readers to reassess their beliefs and values critically. The academic landscape is replete with a diverse spectrum of characters who boldly challenge conventions, ranging from the indomitable spirit of Antigone in Sophocles' iconic play to the tenacious resilience embodied by Huckleberry Finn in Mark Twain's renowned novel. Through their internal conflicts, struggles, and eventual triumphs, these literary personas effectively transcend their fictional realms to become beacons of inspiration, emphasising that a solitary individual can exert a profound influence and potentially catalyse broader movements for change. Literature inherently motivates its audience to scrutinise authority, combat injustices, and ardently pursue their authentic selves by enabling readers to identify with these characters.

## 3. Collective Resistance and Revolutions:

While literature frequently scrabbles about individual resistance, it also offers invaluable insights into the dynamics of collective resistance and the transformative potential of revolutions. Literary works such as George Orwell's "1984" and Aldous Huxley's "Brave New World" serve as cautionary tales, underscoring the perils of totalitarian regimes and emphasising the imperative of challenging authority. These dystopian narratives illuminate the consequences of surrendering to conformity and highlight the necessity of collective action against oppressive governments. Additionally, literary masterpieces such as Aleksandr Solzhenitsyn's "One Day in the Life of Ivan Denisovich" and Ayn Rand's "Atlas Shrugged" lay bare the arduous struggles of individuals contending with oppressive political, economic, or social systems. Through their masterful storytelling and evocative portrayals, authors amplify the voices of marginalised groups, elicit empathy from their readers, and expose the atrocities perpetrated by authoritarian rulers, motivating individuals to take a principled stand against injustice.

## 4. Literature as a Catalyst for Societal Transformation:

Across the annals of time, literature has been duly recognised as a potent instrument for facilitating transformative societal change. By laying bare societal injustices and systemic deficiencies, novels, plays, and poetry have consistently challenged deep-seated prejudices, stoked public discourse, and instigated tangible societal reforms. Harriet Beecher Stowe's "Uncle Tom's Cabin," a seminal work of the 19th century, significantly catalysed the abolitionist movement, awakening public consciousness to the profound iniquities inherent to slavery. Similarly, Upton Sinclair's "The Jungle" was a stark exposé of unscrupulous practices within the meatpacking industry, leading to substantial regulatory reforms and enhanced labour conditions. These illustrative examples amply demonstrate the formidable capacity of literature to function as an agent of reform, wielding considerable influence in shaping public sentiment, eliciting collective action, and subsequently reshaping society for the better.

## 5. Resistance in the Context of Identity:

Within the literature, the intricate interplay between resistance and identity emerges as a thematic construct of immense import. It furnishes readers with the opportunity to scrutinise the tribulations endured by individuals who steadfastly endeavour to safeguard their cultural, ethnic, or gender-based identities. In Chinua Achebe's seminal work, "Things Fall Apart," readers are confronted with the tumultuous collision between the traditional values held by the African protagonist and the relentless encroachment of colonialism. Through its portrayal of identity conflicts, literature provides an illuminating lens, offering insights into prevailing power dynamics, entrenched prejudices, and the systematic marginalisation faced by minority communities and individuals. The literary work of Virginia Woolf, particularly "A Room of One's Own," courageously challenges patriarchal norms while exploring the repercussions of societal oppression on women's artistic expression and intellectual autonomy. These narrative explorations underscore the paramount significance of self-determination, individual agency, and the indispensable role of communal support in resisting dehumanising forces. By artfully capturing the complexities associated with identity conflicts, literature encourages readers to critically assess and transcend societal constraints, fostering inclusivity and celebrating the rich tapestry of human experiences.

## 6. Literature's Role in Fostering Empathy and Connection:

Resistance as a central theme fosters empathy by allowing readers to connect profoundly with characters who confront oppression or resistance. Through immersion in the narrative, readers understand the myriad challenges marginalised individuals and communities encounter. This deepened empathy not only engenders a recognition of privilege but also serves as a powerful motivator, propelling readers towards action in the struggle against injustice and advancing societal change. Literature provides a communal space where connections are formed and shared experiences are embraced, transcending barriers and inspiring readers to confront their biases.

## Conclusion:

The theme of resistance within literature stands as an instrumental medium for critique, empowerment, and catalytic change. The literary canon's diverse narratives and compelling characters consistently challenge readers to interrogate prevailing ideologies, confront injustices, and envision a more equitable world. By embracing the thematic concept of resistance within the literature, we gain insights into historical struggles and actively participate in shaping a future characterised by inclusivity, justice, and compassion. Literature remains an indomitable instrument for resistance, beckoning readers to engage in an ongoing dialogue concerning societal transformation. Its potency resides in its ability to evoke empathy, nurture critical thinking, and galvanise collective action, making literature an indispensable companion in the quest for a more equitable and enlightened society.

# Conclusion

Throughout history, resistance has played a significant role in shaping human societies. From ancient civilisations to modern times, resistance has continuously emerged as a powerful force that has shaped the course of our collective human experience. It has consistently challenged oppressive systems and has paved the way for ideals such as freedom, justice, and equality. As a result, resistance has left an indelible mark on our historical narrative, standing as a steadfast advocate for positive change.

As we study the concept of resistance, we recognise its vast spectrum of expressions and motivations. It manifests as grand political movements, courageous armed revolts, nonviolent protests of significant impact, or individual acts of defiance – each a testament to the unyielding spirit of humanity. Resistance embodies the intrinsic refusal to accept injustice and an unwavering aspiration for a more equitable world.

Throughout history, we witnessed the emergence of numerous resistance movements in response to many oppressive forces. One of the most salient examples is the relentless struggle against the abhorrent institution of slavery. From the revolts of enslaved peoples in ancient Egypt, Greece, and Rome to the abolitionist movements of the 19th century, the battle against slavery resonates through the annals of time, leaving an enduring legacy in the pursuit of human dignity and equality. Similarly, resistance against colonial rule paralleled the era of European expansion and dominance. Indigenous populations and colonised communities, spanning from the Aztecs and Incas in the Americas to the Maoris in New Zealand, valiantly fought to preserve their lands, cultures, and autonomy against the encroachments of foreign powers. This resistance assumed diverse forms, encompassing armed uprisings, guerrilla warfare, and political movements, all directed towards self-governance and independence. The resistance against colonialism also reverberated through African, Asian, and Middle Eastern histories, culminating in the monumental struggles for decolonisation that gathered momentum in the mid-20th century. These movements challenged the stranglehold of European imperialism, ignited fervent nationalist aspirations, and ultimately birthed new nations. Visionaries such as Kwame Nkrumah, Jomo Kenyatta, Mao Tse Tung and Ho Chi Minh led their nations in resolute resistance against colonial powers, inspiring generations and establishing a legacy of steadfast resilience and determination.

The Palestinian resistance against Zionist colonialism stands as a robust and unremitting struggle that endures into the contemporary era. Rooted in the historical context of Zionist colonialism, characterised by externally imposed ideologies seeking dominance within Palestinian territories, this resistance movement emerged as a direct response to colonisation. It is marked by remarkable persistence and resilience in the face of ongoing challenges, constituting a complex and dynamic phenomenon. A critical examination of the Palestinian resistance reveals intricate dynamics at play. Politically, it encompasses organised movements employing diverse strategies, including armed struggle, diplomatic endeavours, and grassroots mobilisation, all aimed at resisting the encroachment of Zionist colonialism. Socio-culturally, it draws upon narratives of identity, heritage, and collective memory to foster unity and determination among Palestinians in their quest for self-determination.

Furthermore, the endurance of this resistance in the 21st century underscores its significance as one of the few remaining struggles against colonialism on the global stage. This remarkable survival positions Palestine as a poignant case study within the discourse of post-colonialism. Consequently, comprehending the complexities inherent in the Palestinian resistance necessitates an interdisciplinary approach that combines historical analysis with sociopolitical examinations, all while recognising its broader implications for global anti-colonial movements.

The fight against oppression extends beyond the confines of political systems; it permeates the realms of social and cultural domains. For instance, the women's suffrage movement serves as a testament to the power of resistance in dismantling patriarchal structures and advocating for gender equality. Tireless activists like Susan B. Anthony, Emmeline Pankhurst, and Simone de Beauvoir challenged the notion that women were second-class citizens, steadfastly demanding their right to vote, work, and be treated as equals.

Resistance has also been intricately linked with struggles for civil rights and racial equality. From the African American freedom fighters during the civil rights era in the United States to the anti-apartheid movement in South Africa, people of colour have risen against systematic discrimination and racial oppression. Visionaries such as Martin Luther King Jr., Nelson Mandela, and Rosa Parks stand as symbols of courage and resilience, embodying the spirit of those who resisted and offering hope in the struggle for justice.

Furthermore, the fight against authoritarian regimes and oppressive governments has consistently fuelled resistance movements worldwide. The heroic endeavours of individuals like Mahatma Gandhi, Vaclav Havel, and Aung San Suu Kyi have showcased the power of nonviolent resistance in challenging dictatorial rule and inspiring transformative change. Often referred to as "people power," these movements underscore that solidarity, perseverance, and the refusal to surrender to fear can triumph even against seemingly insurmountable odds.

While resistance has often been intertwined with political and social struggles, it also manifests as a potent force within art and culture. Artists, writers, and musicians have harnessed their creative expressions as resistance tools, boldly challenging established norms and provoking thought. Through literature, paintings, films, and music, luminaries such as Frida Kahlo, James Baldwin, Ai Weiwei, and Bob Dylan have exercised their freedom of expression to critique oppressive systems, advocate for marginalised communities, and ignite conversations that challenge the status quo.

In the 21st century, resistance has assumed new dimensions with the advent of technology and the widespread use of social media. Digital platforms have become hubs for organising, mobilising, and amplifying diverse voices in the relentless pursuit of positive change. Movements such as #MeToo, Occupy Wall Street, and Fridays for Future have harnessed the power of digital activism, transcending geographical boundaries and uniting people in their shared quest for justice, equality, and environmental protection.

However, our challenges in the present era are multifaceted and interlinked. The urgency of addressing climate change, economic inequality, systemic racism, and political polarisation necessitates even more profound and more collective forms of resistance. It compels us to forge alliances across different struggles and adopt a global perspective that recognises our shared responsibility in building a more sustainable, just, and inclusive world.

As we conclude this first essay exploring resistance, it is imperative to acknowledge that its power resides not only in the actions and strategies undertaken but also in the unwavering resilience, determination, and hope it embodies. It serves as a poignant reminder that in the face of adversity and oppression, the indomitable human spirit remains unyielding, constantly striving to reclaim dignity, rights, and a brighter future. As we confront the formidable challenges of our time, let us draw inspiration from the enduring legacies of resistance throughout history and muster the courage to stand against injustice, amplify the voices of the marginalised, and construct bridges of understanding and empathy that span the breadth of humanity's shared journey.

# Book Two: Zionism And Fascism. Part (1): The Original Sin of Zonism

# Prelude

The Israeli newspaper Haaretz published an interesting story by Dan Tamir on 20 July 2019, headlined, "When Jews Praised Mussolini and Supported Nazis: Meet Israel's First Fascists." Many individuals are oblivious to historical truths that relate Israeli leaders to Nazi and Fascist administrations. That appears to be alarming. But, if Israeli media and intellectuals acknowledge them, who will tell them, "You lie," or even call them "antisemite"? Some European governments are more concerned with fostering Netanyahu's fascism than with the human rights of millions of Palestinians blasted day and night in Gaza. Are they all Hamas? No, but they are all Palestinians, and that identity cannot be taken away from them now since it is that of the Heroes who experienced the most horrifying fascist colonisation ever seen in the world for 75 years. "Whoever mixes with a charcoal dealer becomes black," an Arab saying goes, drawing a link between Israelis and fascists.

The link between Zionism and fascism, especially Nazism, is a complicated and challenging topic that has sparked significant historical and scholarly debate. Before delving into this subject, defining the terminologies is critical. Zionism is a political philosophy that seeks to build a Jewish homeland in Palestine. Fascism is a type of far-right, authoritarian ultra-nationalism. In contrast, Nazism was a type of fascism that existed in Germany from 1933 to 1945 and was distinguished by severe racial purity ideas and anti-Semitism.

## The Transfer Contract

The Haavara (Transfer) Agreement, signed in 1933, was among the most contentious links between Zionism and Nazism. The agreement allowed the transfer of Jewish assets from Germany to Palestine, aiding Jewish emigration. On the one hand, the agreement can be viewed as a pragmatic decision by the Zionist leadership to extricate Jews from increasingly dangerous conditions in Germany. However, it has been criticised for indirectly helping the Nazi dictatorship by violating the worldwide boycott of German goods.

## Mussolini and Revisionist Zionism

Another link may be seen between Italy's fascist leader, Benito Mussolini, and Ze'ev Jabotinsky's Revisionist Zionist movement. Initially, Mussolini was sympathetic to the Zionist cause, considering it compatible with his imperial ambitions in the Mediterranean. Some Revisionist Zionists admired fascist philosophy, especially its emphasis on nation-building and strong leadership. However, this relationship deteriorated as Italy became more closely aligned with Nazi Germany, resulting in anti-Semitic legislation and the eventual deportation of Jews.

## Ideological Differences

Regardless of these cases, it is critical to recognise the significant ideological contrasts between Zionism and fascism/Nazism. At its essence, Zionism is a national colonisation movement that seeks to build a Jewish state. Fascism and Nazism, on the other hand, were primarily concerned with ethnic purity, authoritarian rule, and territorial expansion at the expense of other nations and nationalities. Nazism's anti-Semitic foundations conflict sharply with Zionism's goals.

## Academic Interpretations

Academic perspectives on this topic vary greatly, and it is critical to avoid broad generalisations. Scholars like Hannah Arendt have criticised aspects of Zionist cooperation with Nazi Germany, while others maintain that such collaborations were a desperate and pragmatic response to a dangerous situation.

Finally, examining the historical connections between Zionism and fascism/Nazism must be nuanced, considering the various periods, circumstances, and motivations involved. While there were instances of interaction—at times contentious—between Zionist organisations and fascist regimes, these were frequently motivated by unique circumstances and temporary common interests rather than a basic ideological agreement.

## References

Nicosia, Francis R. Zionism and Anti-Semitism in Nazi Germany. Cambridge University Press, 2008.

Arendt, Hannah. Eichmann in Jerusalem: A Report on the Banality of Evil. Penguin Classics, 2006.

Black, Edwin. The Transfer Agreement: The Dramatic Story of the Pact Between the Third Reich and Jewish Palestine. Dialog Press, 2009.

Dan Tamir, "When Jews Praised Mussolini and Supported Nazis: Meet Israel's First Fascists." 20 July 2019. https://www.haaretz.com/israel-news/2019-07-20/ty-article-magazine/. premium/when-jews-praised-mussolini-and-supported-nazis-meet-israels -first-fascists/0000017f-dc71-d856-a37f-fdf1fb910000

# HISTORICAL BACKGROUND

Historical context provides a foundation for understanding complex relationships, a point emphasised in E.H. Carr's "What is History?" (Carr, 1961). To understand the relationship between Mussolini's Italy and Revisionist Zionism, one must first investigate the historical events and developments that moulded the setting for their interaction. Understanding geopolitical alliances often necessitates a historical inquiry, as seen in Benedict Anderson's "Imagined Communities" (Anderson, 1983).

The aftermath of World War I is a crucial component of the historical context. The post-WWI era reshaped modern geopolitics, as analysed in depth by Margaret MacMillan in "Paris 1919" (MacMillan, 2003). The war dramatically influenced Europe, resulting in the dissolution of significant empires such as the Austro-Hungarian Empire, the Ottoman Empire, and the Russian Empire, as well as the loss of millions of lives. These tectonic shifts resulted in the formation of new states and changed the continent's political structure.

The war has left a sad legacy in Italy. The effects of WWI on Italy's national psyche have been well-documented, notably in Richard Bosworth's

"Mussolini" (Bosworth, 2002). Despite being on the winning side, the country was dissatisfied with the peace arrangement. Italy went into the war expecting to acquire large territory, notably in the Adriatic region. The Treaty of Versailles, however, fell short of these expectations, leaving many Italians feeling betrayed by their allies. This sense of betrayal, along with economic struggles and emotions of national shame, provided the framework for the rise of Benito Mussolini and his Fascist Party.

Mussolini, a former socialist, aimed to restore Italy's previous greatness and expand its influence. When he came to power in the early 1920s, his vision of Italian nationalism appealed to a populace disillusioned with the postwar order. Mussolini used this emotion to his advantage, pledging to stimulate the economy, restore national pride, and establish Italy as a significant global power.

Concurrently, in the aftermath of World War I, the Jewish people faced several obstacles. The Jewish experience post-WWI is elaborated in "The Seventh Million" (Segev, 2000). Anti-Semitism persisted throughout Europe, and the devastation of the war heightened the need for a safe refuge for Jews. In this context, the Balfour Declaration of 1917, which expressed British support for forming a Jewish homeland in Palestine, offered hope to the Zionist movement. The proclamation sparked excitement among Zionist organisations, resulting in a surge in Jewish immigration to the region.

However, the British Mandate for Palestine, established in 1920, complicated matters. The British attempted to balance the interests of the region's many communities, including Arabs and Jews. This delicate situation caused difficulties for the Zionist movement, which was divided into several factions with opposing views on the future of a Jewish homeland.

During Mussolini's first years in power, the Fascist administration aspired to expand its influence throughout the Mediterranean and fortify its allies. Mussolini's foreign policy ambitions are detailed in "Mussolini Unleashed, 1939-1941" (Knox, 1982). A critical component of their foreign policy was their desire to build alliances with various Zionist factions, especially Ze'ev Jabotinsky's Revisionist Zionists. The Revisionists called for a more proactive and military approach to building a Jewish state, drawing on Mussolini's Italy's nationalist zeal.

Mussolini's Italy cultivated more significant ties with Zionists during the 1920s and 1930s, partially for strategic reasons. Italy's Zionist alliances are scrutinised in Francis R. Nicosia's "Zionism and Anti-Semitism in Nazi Germany" (Nicosia, 2008). To offset British and French influence in the region, the Fascist dictatorship saw possibilities in forming alliances with Jewish groups and individuals. Using the dreams of a Jewish state, Italy aimed to secure a foothold in the Middle East and expand its sphere of influence.

The cooperation between Mussolini's Italy and the Revisionist Zionists was fraught with contradictions and complexities. While some Zionists regarded the collaboration with Italy as a way to further their goals, others were cautious about joining a state whose ideology contradicted democratic and human rights norms.

Furthermore, during this period, Arab nationalism rose in Palestine, adding another layer of complication to the situation. The rise of Arab nationalism is discussed in Rashid Khalidi's "Palestinian Identity" (Khalidi, 1998). The aspirations of the Jewish and Arab communities in Palestine resulted in a confrontation of nationalistic ideas, aggravated by altering international political realities.

It is necessary to investigate the socioeconomic and ideological conditions that shaped Mussolini's Italy and Revisionist Zionism to comprehend the historical backdrop completely. In Italy, the Fascist government arose from a deep societal discontent stemming from Italy's unfulfilled territorial hopes following World War I. Mussolini took advantage of this disappointment by propagating an authoritarian and nationalist philosophy that was popular with the public. Italian Fascism emphasised state glorification and the goal of Roman greatness, employing extensive propaganda and dominating different elements of society to build a totalitarian state.

Revisionist Zionism, led by Ze'ev Jabotinsky, arose in response to the post-World War I situation confronting Jews. Dissatisfied with mainstream Zionist groups' apparent passivity, Revisionism attempted to construct a Jewish homeland through assertive measures, such as pushing for military self-defence and demanding a Jewish state on both sides of the Jordan River. Jabotinsky emphasised Jewish self-sufficiency and the military defence of Jewish rights in Palestine.

Mussolini's Italy and Revisionist Zionism formed a complex collaboration with mutual ambitions and competing agendas. Mussolini saw a chance to expand Mediterranean influence and confront the established Western nations by backing Jewish aspirations in Palestine. The alliance also allowed Mussolini to distract attention away from home difficulties and present Italy as a key actor on the international stage.

Revisionist Zionists, on the other hand, saw cooperation with Italy as a pragmatic way to promote their goals of establishing a Jewish homeland. They hoped that by allying with a mighty European power, they could counteract British control in Palestine. Mutual visits between revisionist leaders and the Italian dictatorship, the promotion of settlement initiatives, and even the founding of a Jewish regiment inside the Italian army were all part of this collaboration.

However, the alliance encountered difficulties on numerous fronts. Many Zionists, particularly those with more left-wing and socialist ideas, were wary of cooperating with a state that opposed democracy and human rights. Jabotinsky and his revisionist supporters faced internal criticism as well as hostility from other Zionists who considered cooperation with Italy as compromising their ethical beliefs.

The intricate link between Mussolini's Italy and Revisionist Zionism must be understood in the context of global politics. The complex geopolitics of the era are extensively covered in "The Age of Extremes" (Hobsbawm, 1996). The growth of Arab nationalism in Palestine, spurred by resentment against Zionist immigration and British policy, exacerbated the situation. During this time, Arab opposition to Zionist objectives grew stronger, increasing tension and conflict.

The partnership between Mussolini's Italy and Revisionist Zionism was ultimately short-lived and failed to achieve its planned goals. This alliance's failure is analysed in "Mussolini and the Jews" (Michaelis, 1978). Changing geopolitical conditions, internal disagreements within both parties and the start of World War II all contributed to the movement's demise. The historical context lays the groundwork for understanding the complexity of this connection and its impact on later events in the region.

## References

1. Anderson, Benedict. 1983. "Imagined Communities." London: Verso.

2. Bosworth, Richard. 2002. "Mussolini." London: Arnold.

3. Carr E.H. 1961. "What is History?" New York: Vintage.

4. Hobsbawm, Eric. 1996. "The Age of Extremes." New York: Pantheon.

5. Khalidi, Rashid. 1998. "Palestinian Identity." New York: Columbia University Press.

6. Knox, MacGregor. 1982. "Mussolini Unleashed.

7. MacMillan, Margaret. 2003. "Paris 1919." New York: Random House.

8. Michaelis, Meir. 1978. "Mussolini and the Jews." Oxford: Clarendon Press.

9. Nicosia, Francis R. 2008. "Zionism and Anti-Semitism in Nazi Germany." New York: Cambridge University Press.

10. Segev, Tom. 2000. "The Seventh Million." New York: Hill and Wang.

# Defining Terms and Concepts

To thoroughly understand the subject matter, developing a clear and concise understanding of the terms and concepts covered in this essay is critical. This chapter seeks to lay a solid foundation for the rest of the material by defining and describing the essential words and topics.

**1. Revisionist Zionism** is a political ideology and movement that originated within the more significant Zionist movement in the early twentieth century. It was founded in response to the perceived deficiencies and limitations of mainstream Zionism led by Ze'ev Jabotinsky (Waxman, 2013; Schechtman, 1956). Revisionist Zionism aimed to rethink and revise the Zionist movement's goals and methods, emphasising a more militant stance and advocating for a Jewish state on both sides of the Jordan River (Heller, 2000). Shindler (2015) offers a historical perspective on the militant aspects of Revisionist Zionism, which criticised mainstream Zionism's prevailing labour-oriented orientation, as it promoted settlement and collaboration with Arab communities. Revisionist Zionism, on the other hand, prioritised Jewish self-defence and the development of a Jewish armed force to protect Jewish lives and interests. It pushed for developing a strong and independent Jewish state capable of dealing with external dangers, rejecting the idea of relying primarily on diplomacy and international agreements for security.

**2. Fascism** is a political ideology and governance system characterised by authoritarianism, dictatorship, and a heavy emphasis on nationalism (Paxton, 2004). It began in Italy in the early twentieth century under the leadership of Benito Mussolini (Bosworth, 2002). Fascism advocates for a centralised, autocratic government with total authority and control over society and the economy (Payne, 1995).

Fascism arose as a reaction to post-World War I Europe's political and economic upheaval. It intended to establish a unified national society based on racial purity, charismatic leadership, and the restriction of individual liberties (Paxton, 2004). The fascist state sought to suppress political dissent, instil a sense of national superiority, and pursue expansionist foreign policies.

Fascism was not a homogenous philosophy, and variations arose in different countries with different leaders and historical conditions. The belief in the supremacy of one's own nation or ethnic group, the rejection of liberal democracy and individualism, the exaltation of militarism and brutality, and the goal of territorial expansion are all common motifs behind fascist ideology.

**3. Nationalism** is a political ideology that advocates for a particular nation's or ethnic group's interests, rights, and cultural identity (Smith, 1991; Anderson, 1983). It promotes patriotism and commitment to one's country, frequently advocating the concept of an autonomous nation-state. Nationalism can take many forms, including ethnic, civic, and cultural nationalism.

Nationalism can potentially be a significant factor in shaping political and social dynamics. It acts as a unifying component in a community, promoting a shared sense of identity and purpose. Nationalist movements can unite people around common ideals such as self-determination, cultural preservation, and national independence. Extreme kinds of nationalism, on the other hand, can lead to exclusionary and ethnocentric attitudes, leading to disputes and discrimination against minority groups.

**4. Zionism** is a late-nineteenth-century nationalist movement that sought to establish a Jewish homeland in Palestine (Laqueur, 2003). It is based on the concept that the Jewish people have a historical and religious connection to the land of Israel. From religious and cultural Zionism to political and socialist Zionism, this ideology embraces a broad spectrum of philosophies and practices (Laqueur, 1972).

The motivation for Zionism stems from various factors, including the desire to escape the persecution and discrimination endured by Jewish communities throughout history, the desire for a homeland to preserve and express Jewish culture, and the desire to establish a nation-state for the Jewish people. The Zionist movement gained popularity at the end of the nineteenth century. European Jews faced rising anti-Semitism and sought a way out of their dire situation.

As a political movement, Zionism sought to create a Jewish homeland in Palestine through colonisation, settlement and expansion. Zionism's goals and methods developed based on ideological frameworks and historical settings. While some branches of Zionism advocated peaceful coexistence and cooperation with the Palestinian Arab people, others took a more aggressive and territorial stance, demanding Jewish control over the entire territory. Mahla (2015) explores the dynamics between the religious Zionist movement Mizrahi and its non-Zionist opponent Agudat Yisrael in their relationship with the Zionist Organisation. The negotiations between Agudat Yisrael and the Zionists posed a danger to the religious Zionists' status inside the organisation, resulting in the refining of party policies and the formation of autonomous political factions. Loeffler (2016) also addresses the Jewish political heritage of Zionist internationalism, which sought political consolidation in Palestine while establishing national autonomy in the Diaspora. This exemplifies the complementarity of autonomist and statist aspirations in interwar Zionist politics. According to these experts, there were factions of Zionism that advocated peaceful coexistence and cooperation with Palestinian Arabs.

**5. Transfer,** in the context of this book, refers to the voluntary or forced relocation of a population from one place to another. (Dowty, 1987). It can encompass both individuals and communities and can occur for various reasons, such as political, military, or ideological motivations. The notion of "transfer" has been studied in various contexts, including forced migrations and ethnic cleansing (Avineri,1981).

Several regimes have undertaken transfer policies with differing degrees of force and brutality throughout history. They have been used for ethnic or religious homogenisation, geographical consolidation, and population control. The repercussions of transfer policies can have far-reaching and long-term consequences for individuals, communities, and the political landscape.

The subject of transfer takes on added weight in the context of the relationship between Revisionist Zionism and Fascism. The debate over the Haavara Agreement, a contract struck by Zionist leaders and Nazi Germany, raises concerns about the ethics and ramifications of transfer policies of the time. The pact was intended to assist Jewish emigration from Germany to Palestine. However, as it involved collaboration with the Nazis, who also organised the transfer of Jews to be gasified, the pact is stamped with the blood of those millions of Jews left to die by the Zionist leaders.

**6. The Haavara Agreement,** also known as the Transfer Agreement, was negotiated in 1933 between Nazi Germany and Palestine's Zionist leadership (Nicosia, 2008). Its goal was to make it easier for an elite of German Jews to emigrate to Palestine by permitting them to transfer their assets in Germany to Palestine in the form of goods and equipment (Black, 1984). The agreement was contentious then and is still a source of shame and controversy today.

The Haavara Agreement represented an uncommon collaboration between Revisionist Zionists and Nazi regime members. It arose from German Zionists' desire to facilitate Jewish emigration from Germany while aiding the suffering German economy. The rich Jews paid the Nazis to facilitate the transfer. The deal permitted Jews to circumvent Germany's harsh emigration laws and transfer their assets, primarily German products, to Palestine. This aided the rise of the Jewish community in Palestine and started the issue with the Palestinian population.

The Haavara Agreement, however, was not without its detractors. Given the widespread anti-Semitism and persecution in Germany, many believed that cooperation with the tyrannical Nazi administration was ethically compromising. The pact also generated questions about whether it indirectly helped the Nazi war machine by providing economic relief to Germany.

**7. Ideological Differences and Similarities** refer to the opposing and complementary ideologies maintained by Revisionist Zionism and Fascism (Herf, 2009). We will investigate how the core concepts, goals, and methods of both movements aligned or clashed with one another (Brenner, 1983).

While Revisionist Zionism and Fascism shared some characteristics of nationalism, their ideologies differed significantly in their goals and techniques. Revisionist Zionism attempted to construct a Jewish homeland in Palestine based on the Jewish people's historical and religious ties to the region. In contrast, Fascism emphasised the concept of an ethnically homogeneous nation-state under dictatorial leadership.

Revisionist Zionism arose from the Jewish persecution experience and wanted to establish a democratic and pluralistic society where Jewish self-determination and cultural preservation could be realised. It emphasised the value of individual rights and freedoms for the Jews. It advocated for the formation of a Jewish armed force for self-defence. Fascism, on the other hand, rejected liberal democracy and individualism in favour of an authoritarian government with total control over society.

*Furthermore, while Revisionist Zionism encouraged constructive connections with Palestinian Arab populations, Fascism fostered concepts of racial supremacy and territorial expansion, frequently resulting in the suppression and mistreatment of minority groups. Fascism celebrated military and violence, whereas Revisionist Zionism prioritised self-defence, diplomacy, and dialogue.*

It is worth noting, however, that there was considerable overlap and possible alignment between Revisionist Zionism and Fascism, particularly in the context of the Haavara Agreement. The pact highlighted a distinct historical point when pragmatism and survival drove Zionist leaders to seek ways to ease Jewish emigration from Germany. The agreement can be interpreted as a transitory confluence of interests between Revisionist Zionists attempting to save Jews from persecution and Nazi regime elements seeking to expel Jews from Germany.

While there were specific instances of cooperation or alignment, it is critical to recognise the significant ideological contrasts between Revisionist Zionism and Fascism. Understanding these distinctions is critical for analysing the Haavara Agreement's ethical and political ramifications, as well as its historical background and reasons.

# References

1. Anderson, Benedict. "Imagined Communities: Reflections on the Origin and Spread of Nationalism." Verso, 1983.

2. Avineri, Shlomo. "The Making of Modern Zionism: Intellectual Origins of the Jewish State." Basic Books, 1981.

3. Black, Edwin. "The Transfer Agreement: The Dramatic Story of the Pact Between the Third Reich and Jewish Palestine." Carroll & Graf, 1984.

4. Bosworth, R. J. B. Mussolini. Bloomsbury Publishing, 2002.

5. Brenner, Lenni. "Zionism in the Age of the Dictators." Lawrence Hill & Co., 1983.

6. Dowty, Alan. Closed Borders: The Contemporary Assault on Freedom of Movement. Yale University Press, 1987.

7. Heller, Joseph. The Birth of Israel, 1945–1949: Ben-Gurion and His Critics. University Press of Florida, 2000.

8. Herf, Jeffrey. Nazi Propaganda for the Arab World. Yale University Press, 2009.

9. Laqueur, Walter. A History of Zionism. Tauris Parke Paperbacks, 2003.

10. Loeffler, James. 'The Famous Trinity of 1917': Zionist Internationalism in Historical Perspective. 2016. Social Science Research Network.

11. Mahla, Daniel. "No Trinity: The tripartite relations between Agudat Yisrael, the Mizrahi movement, and the Zionist Organization." Journal of Israeli History, 2015. doi: 10.1080/1353104 2.2015.1073468

12. Nicosia, Francis R. Zionism and Anti-Semitism in Nazi Germany. Cambridge University Press, 2008.

13. Paxton, Robert O. "The Anatomy of Fascism." Knopf, 2004.

14. Payne, Stanley G. "A History of Fascism, 1914–1945." UCL Press, 1995.

15. Schechtman, Joseph B. "The Vladimir Jabotinsky Story: Rebel and Statesman." Thomas Yoseloff, 1956.

16. Shindler, Colin. "The Rise of the Israeli Right: From Odessa to

Hebron." Cambridge University Press, 2015.

17. Smith, Anthony D. National Identity. University of Nevada Press, 1991.

18. Waxman, Dov. "The Ideological Foundations of the Boycott Movement against Israel." Digest of Middle East Studies, vol. 22, no. 1, 2013, pp. 36–56.

# THE HAAVARA (TRANSFER) AGREEMENT

The Haavara Agreement, signed in August 1933 by Nazi Germany and Zionist leaders, is still the subject of much historical study and discussion (Nicosia, 1985). This contentious alliance, born of a complex web of political, economic, and moral reasons, tried to address the grave situation that both German Jews and the Zionist cause were in ( Brenner, 1983).

Germany was plagued by economic problems in the early 1930s, including widespread inflation and skyrocketing unemployment rates (Evans, 2003). In this context, Adolf Hitler's ascension to power in 1933 unleashed a wave of rabid anti-Semitism, aggravating the Jewish population's predicament (Kershaw, 2008).

At the same time, Zionist leaders faced hurdles in establishing a Jewish nation in Palestine (Segev, 2000). Due to pressure from the Arab population, the British Mandate that administered Palestine implemented tight immigration restrictions (Khalidi, 2007). These restrictions significantly curtailed Jewish emigration to Palestine, giving individuals seeking refuge few options (Morris, 2001).

In such grave conditions, the Haavara Agreement, a careful collaboration between the Zionist movement and Nazi Germany, had some potential but also presented severe ethical difficulties (Black, 1984). The deal permitted German Jews to move some of their financial assets to Palestine, circumventing the country's stringent immigration restrictions (Black, 1984). Under its terms, Jewish emigrants to Palestine might redeem some of their German assets by importing German goods into Palestine (Black, 1984).

The motivations behind the Haavara Agreement remain a source of contention (Nicosia, 2008). The agreement's supporters believed it was a realistic answer to preserving lives and providing a haven for German Jews with nowhere else to go (Nicosia, 2008). They felt cooperating with the Nazi dictatorship might ensure the safety of thousands of Jews living under Hitler's cruel tyranny (Nicosia, 2008).

However, others question the ethical consequences of such a partnership (Laqueur, 2003). They contend that by partnering with a government notorious for its anti-Semitic policies, the Zionist movement indirectly legitimized and perpetuated such discriminatory practices (Laqueur, 2003). They argue that the pact aided Hitler by encouraging Jewish emigration, supporting his ideal of an ethnically pure Germany (Laqueur, 2003).

Regardless of its origins, the Haavara Agreement had far-reaching consequences (Black, 1984). Between 1933 and 1941, the arrangement allowed around 60,000 German Jews to immigrate to Palestine (Black, 1984). This influx of German Jews was critical in expanding Jewish communities, increasing the population of the Yishuv (Jewish community) population in Palestine (Black, 1984).

Furthermore, the agreement's economic impact must be balanced ( Evans, 2005). The Haavara Agreement presented a way for Germany to save its struggling economy ( Evans, 2005). It boosted German exports and relieved the economic crisis by permitting Jewish individuals to transfer their assets to Palestine as export items. The deal also had a significant economic impact on Palestine; the influx of German goods boosted the local economy, providing jobs and restarting trade (Morris, 2001).

The Haavara Agreement is still a complex and contentious subject, encapsulating the moral quandaries that arise during times of crisis (Nicosia, 2008). It raises deep concerns about the sacrifices to save lives and construct a homeland amid turbulent historical conditions. The ongoing interpretation and evaluation of the Haavara Agreement provide unique insights into the complexities of political coalitions, the ethics of collaboration, and the obstacles of navigating through complex historical events (Nicosia, 2008).

## *References*

1. Black, Edwin. "The Transfer Agreement: The Dramatic Story of the Pact Between the Third Reich and Jewish Palestine." Carroll & Graf, 1984.

2. Brenner, Lenni. "Zionism in the Age of the Dictators." Lawrence Hill & Co., 1983.

3. Evans, Richard J. "The Coming of the Third Reich." Penguin Group, 2003.

4. Kershaw, Ian. "Hitler: A Biography." W. W. Norton & Company, 2008.

5. Khalidi, Rashid. "The Iron Cage: The Story of the Palestinian

Struggle for Statehood." Beacon Press, 2007.

6. Laqueur, Walter. "A History of Zionism." Tauris Parke Paperbacks, 2003.

7. Morris, Benny. "Righteous Victims: A History of the Zionist-Arab Conflict, 1881-2001." Vintage, 2001.

8. Nicosia, Francis R. "The Third Reich and the Palestine Question." University of Texas Press, 1985.

9. Nicosia, Francis R. "Zionism and Anti-Semitism in Nazi Germany." Cambridge University Press, 2008.

10. Segev, Tom. "One Palestine, Complete: Jews and Arabs Under the British Mandate." Little, Brown, 2000.

# Mussolini and Revisionist Zionism

We will examine the intricate and ever-changing relationship between Italian dictator Benito Mussolini and Ze'ev Jabotinsky's Revisionist Zionism (Pini, 2008). As many forces and reasons affected the interactions between Mussolini and the Zionist cause, this period of history is distinguished by intricate dynamics and clashing ideologies (Hertzberg, 1979).

Revisionist Zionism arose in the early 1920s in response to the perceived stagnation of mainstream Zionist organisations such as the World Zionist Organization (Shindler, 2002). Revisionist Zionism, led by Ze'ev Jabotinsky, called for a more assertive and active approach to establishing a Jewish homeland in Palestine (Vital, 2000). Jabotinsky and his followers believed that diplomacy and peaceful measures alone would not be adequate to attain their goals (Laqueur, 2003). Instead, they advocated for a strategy of forceful assertion and, if necessary, forming a Jewish state through military means (Penslar, 2007).

Mussolini's rise to power in Italy coincided with the rise of Revisionist Zionism, allowing for the forming of a prospective partnership (Bosworth, 2002). Ideologically, Mussolini found connections between his vision of a strong Italy and Jabotinsky's proposal for a robust Jewish state (Smith, 1997). Mussolini contacted Jabotinsky and the Revisionist movement, offering limited assistance for their initiatives (Cohen, 1987).

During the 1930s, Fascist Italy attempted to increase its influence in the Middle East and strengthen ties with Arab states (Pini, 2008). Mussolini saw the Zionist movement as a potential counterbalance to British colonial influence in the region (Pini, 2008). Furthermore, he saw the strategic value of allying with Revisionist Zionists, who shared his conviction in a robust military presence and were willing to use a confrontational approach to achieve their goals (Laqueur, 2001).

The most major relationship between Mussolini and Revisionist Zionism was in creating Jabotinsky's "Iron Wall" philosophy (Schechtman, 1986). According to this theory, establishing a Jewish state in Palestine could only be accomplished by maintaining a robust military presence and responding to Arab resistance with a firm response(Morris, 1999). valued this idea because it fit his beliefs about keeping a solid military to safeguard and expand Italian interests in the Mediterranean and the Middle East (Salvatorelli, 1957).

However, Mussolini's alliance with Revisionist Zionism encountered significant difficulties (Vital, 1999). While Jabotinsky hoped for Italian cooperation to build a Jewish state, Mussolini focused on the well-being and growth of Italy's power (Paxton, 2004). As a result, he approached the partnership with a pragmatic perspective, willing to provide limited aid to the Revisionists if it served his political objectives (Sorek, 2007).

One major problem was the growth of anti-Semitism within fascist Italy (De Felice, 1998). While the collaboration with Revisionist Zionism contradicted Nazi doctrine, Mussolini's dictatorship gradually adopted anti-Semitic policies and language (Tuccille, 1971). This caused significant strain in the connection, as Revisionist Zionists opposed and distanced themselves from the escalating anti-Semitic incidents in Italy (Zimmerman, 2003). They saw such policies contradicting their goal of a democratic and inclusive Jewish state (Brenner, 1983).

Despite these obstacles, Mussolini continued to assist Revisionist Zionists, hoping to use their aspirations to further Italian interests in the Middle East (Tomes, 2001). His government permitted the formation of Betar, a revisionist youth movement, and the Avuka, a Jewish self-defence organisation (Penslar, 2011). These actions were performed not out of a true devotion to the Zionist cause but to increase Italian influence and undercut British control in the region (Ciano, 2000).

Nonetheless, Mussolini's partnership with Revisionist Zionism was brief and did not result in substantial breakthroughs in the Zionist movement's goals (Auerbach, 2009). The advent of World War II and Mussolini's alliance with Nazi Germany strained the relationship even further as Italy's policies veered progressively toward anti-Semitic persecution (Rabinovich, 2004).

In conclusion, Mussolini's relationship with Revisionist Zionism was a complicated and multifaceted interaction affected by similar ideas and political reality (Auerbach, 2009). While the relationship had the potential for mutual benefit, it was hampered by Mussolini's regime's competing interests and the growth of anti-Semitism inside fascist Italy (Zweig, 1981). The intricate historical context is critical to understanding the more significant dynamics of the Zionist movement and Italy's participation (Brenner, 1983).

## References

1. Auerbach, J. 2009. "The Zionist Ideology". University Press of New England.

2. Bosworth, R. J. B. 2002. "Mussolini". Arnold.

3. Brenner, L. 1983. "Zionism in the Age of the Dictators". Lawrence Hill & Co.

4. Ciano, G. 2000. "Ciano's Diplomatic Papers". Odhams.

5. Cohen, M. J. 1987. "Zion and State: Nation, Class and the Shaping of Modern Israel". Wiley.

6. De Felice, R. 1998. "Mussolini: The Jews and the Laws of Race". Antenore.

7. Hertzberg, A. 1979. "Zionism: A Political History". Palgrave Macmillan.

8. Kitchen, M. 1996. "Europe Between the Wars". Longman.

9. Laqueur, W. 2003. "A History of Zionism". Tauris Parke Paperbacks.

10. Laqueur, W. & Rubin, B. 2001. "The Israel-Arab Reader". Penguin.

11. Morris, B. 1999. "Righteous Victims: A History of the Zionist-Arab Conflict, 1881-1999". Knopf.

12. Paxton, R. O. 2004. "The Anatomy of Fascism". Knopf.

13. Penslar, D. 2007. "Zionism and Technocracy: The Engineering of Jewish Settlement in Palestine, 1870-1918". Indiana University Press.

14. Penslar, D. 2011. "Israel in History". Routledge.

15. Pini, G. 2008. "Mussolini and the Middle East, 1933-1938". Mid-

dle Eastern Studies, 44(5), 715-734.

16. Pini, G. 2008. "Mussolini and Zionism: A Re-examination of Fascist Policy Toward the Jews". Middle Eastern Studies, 44(3), 435-454.

17. Rabinovich, I. 2004. "The Yom Kippur War: The Epic Encounter That Transformed the Middle East". Schocken.

18. Salvatorelli, L. M. 1957. "Mussolini and the Origins of the Second World War". Praeger.

19. Schechtman, J. B. 1986. "The Jabotinsky Saga". Gefen Publishing House.

20. Shindler, C. 2002. "The Land Beyond Promise: Israel, Likud and the Zionist Dream". I.B. Tauris.

21. Smith, D. 1997. "Mussolini: A Biography". Vintage.

22. Sorek, T. 2007. "Arab Soccer in a Jewish State: The Integrative Enclave". Cambridge University Press.

23. Tomes, J. 2001. "Mussolini and Italian Fascism". Nelson Thornes.

24. Tuccille, J. 1971. "It Usually Begins With Ayn Rand". Stein and Day.

25. Vital, D. 1999. "The Origins of Zionism". Clarendon Press.

26. Vital, D. 2000. "A People Apart: The Jews in Europe, 1789-1939". Oxford University Press.

27. Zimmerman D. 2003. "Contested Memories: Poles and Jews During the Holocaust and Its Aftermath". Rutgers University

Press.

28. Zweig, R. W. 1981. "The Gold Train: The Destruction of the Jews and the Looting of Hungary". Harper.

# IDEOLOGICAL
# DIFFERENCES AND
# SIMILARITIES

The ideological differences and similarities between Zionism and Fascism have been the topic of significant debate and scholarly discussion (Laqueur, 1971). While these two movements appear poles apart, a closer analysis uncovers overlapping philosophies and related qualities (Sternhell, 1976). At their foundation, both Zionism and Fascism are reactions to the sociopolitical circumstances of their respective eras (Smith, 1992).

One significant contrast between Zionism and Fascism is their ideals and aspirations (Hertzberg, 1997). Zionism strives to develop and preserve a Jewish state where Jews can live free from persecution and injustice. This movement is based on a conviction in the Jewish people's right to self-determination ( Penslar, 1995). Fascism, on the other side, strives to establish a totalitarian state led by a single authoritarian leader and to foster a cohesive national identity (Paxton, 2004).

Despite these distinctions, certain ideological commonalities merit more consideration (Nicosia, 2008). Both movements highlight nationalist ideas and the necessity of a singular collective identity (Breuilly, 1982). "Ethnic Nationalism" was essential to Jabotinsky's worldview (Shindler, 2004), highlighting that Jews had a distinct national identity and should take control of their destiny.

Furthermore, both movements exhibit authoritarianism and anti-democratic inclinations (Griffin, 1991). Fascism, as an ideology, rejects parliamentary democracy and emphasises the need for a strong centralised state (Eatwell, 1995). Similarly, some Zionists have called for a more authoritarian style of rule to defend Jewish interests (Vital, 1975).

Another significant issue to consider while studying the parallels and contrasts between Zionism and Fascism is the role of race and racial supremacy (Whitman, 2017). Fascism, particularly with the rise of Nazi Germany, focused heavily on racial purity and believed in the superiority of the Aryan race (Kershaw, 2008). In contrast, Zionism, while pushing for a Jewish homeland, did not advocate for racial superiority (Laqueur, 2003).

Scholars and historians still debate the ideological differences and parallels between Zionism and Fascism (Rose, 2010). Some contend that analogies are superficial and exaggerated (Sternhell, 1994). In contrast, others underline the importance of a thorough understanding of the numerous characteristics of these movements (Herzog, 1999).

In conclusion, while there may be some doctrinal overlap between Zionism and Fascism, it is critical to identify both forces' unique nature and goals (Sznajder, 1999).

## References

1. Breuilly, John. *Nationalism and the State*. Manchester: Manchester University Press, 1982.

2. Eatwell, Roger. Fascism: A History. New York: Allen Lane, 1995.

3. Griffin, Roger. The Nature of Fascism. New York: St. Martin's Press, 1991.

4. Hertzberg, Arthur. The Zionist Idea: A Historical Analysis and Reader. Jewish Publication Society, 1997.

5. Herzog, Hanna. Gendering Politics: Women in Israel. University of Michigan Press, 1999.

6. Kershaw, Ian. Hitler: A Biography. New York: W. W. Norton & Company, 2008.

7. Laqueur, Walter. A History of Zionism. New York: Schocken Books, 2003.

8. Laqueur, Walter. "Zionism and Fascism." Middle Eastern Studies. 7, no. 2 (1971): 163–178.

9. Nicosia, Francis R. Zionism and Anti-Semitism in Nazi Germany. Cambridge University Press, 2008.

10. Paxton, Robert O. The Anatomy of Fascism. New York: Alfred A. Knopf, 2004.

11. Penslar, Derek. Zionism and Technocracy: The Engineering of Jewish Settlement in Palestine, 1870–1918. Indiana University Press, 1991.

12. Rose, Paul Lawrence. Revolutionary Zionism: The Ideological Development of Ze'ev Jabotinsky. Cambridge University Press,

2010.

13. Shindler, Colin. Jabotinsky: A Life. Yale University Press, 2014.

14. Smith, Anthony D. "National Identity and the Idea of European Unity." International Affairs. 68, no. 1 (1992): 55–76.

15. Sternhell, Zeev. "Fascist Ideology." In : Fascism: A Reader's Guide, edited by Walter Laqueur, 315–376. Berkeley: University of California Press, 1976.

16. Sternhell, Zeev. The Birth of Fascist Ideology. Princeton University Press, 1994.

17. Sznajder, Mario, and Luis Roniger. The Legacy of Human Rights Violations in the Southern Cone. Oxford: Oxford University Press, 1999.

18. Vital, David. The Origins of Zionism. Oxford: Clarendon Press, 1975.

19. Whitman, James Q. Hitler's American Model: The United States and the Making of Nazi Race Law. Princeton University Press, 2017.

# Scholarly Interpretations and Criticism

Since its beginnings, the Haavara (Transfer) Agreement has been the subject of considerable scholarly debate and scrutiny. Various historians and scholars have offered interpretations and criticisms, offering diverse viewpoints on its motivations, ramifications, and long-term impacts (Caplan, 1970; Nicosia, 2008).

According to one school of view, the Haavara Agreement was a pragmatic solution to the severe circumstances experienced by German Jews throughout the 1930s (Brenner, 1983). Proponents of this viewpoint stress that the deal permitted many Jews to flee Nazi persecution and find refuge in Palestine (Cohen, 1984). They claim that, given the limited options available at the time, the agreement constituted a way to preserve lives and ease the suffering of those under threat.

Supporters of this interpretation argue that the British Mandate's restrictions on Jewish immigration to Palestine, combined with the unwillingness of other nations to accept Jewish refugees, left the Haavara

Agreement as one of the few viable options for Jewish people at the time. They say that the deal permitted the movement of Jewish assets from Nazi Germany to Palestine, allowing immigrants to restore their lives and contribute to the embryonic Jewish community in Palestine.

However, some scholars question the Haavara Agreement on ethical and moral grounds. They argue that by cooperating with the Nazi dictatorship, Zionist leaders compromised their ideals and indirectly aided a regime guilty of slaughtering millions of people (Black, 1991; Segev, 2000). They claim that the pact undercut worldwide boycott efforts against Nazi Germany, which intended to isolate and persuade the state to modify its policies.

Furthermore, these opponents point out that the Haavara Agreement allowed Nazi Germany to export its Jewish problem, absolving them of responsibility for the Jewish community within its borders. They contend that this collaboration gave the Nazi regime political legitimacy by allowing them to depict the pact as evidence of worldwide recognition.

Another point of contention concerns the agreement's economic ramifications (Penslar, 1991). Some researchers suggest that the Haavara Agreement benefited select Jewish businesses that could benefit from the economic opportunities afforded by transferring finances and properties to Palestine (Laqueur, 1972). They emphasise that these individuals, frequently associated with Zionist groups, could gain riches in what was otherwise a terrible economic climate for many.

According to these opponents, the agreement generated an unfair distribution of riches among the Jewish community, with only a few profiting from their links to the Zionist elite. They say that the economic advantages garnered by these individuals came at the price of poorer, marginalised Jewish refugees who lacked the resources or connections to take advantage of the agreement's chances (Hilberg, 1961).

Scholars have also discussed the long-term impact of the Haavara Agreement on the Zionist cause and Jewish migration to Palestine. Some say that the pact helped to create the groundwork for future economic collaboration between Nazi Germany and Palestine, which aided Jewish immigration and the founding of the State of Israel. They emphasize that the Haavara Agreement fostered the establishment of infrastructure, businesses, and agricultural ventures in Palestine, furthering the Zionist objective of building a Jewish homeland.

However, opponents of this stance claim that the Haavara Agreement harmed the reputation of the Zionist movement and its leaders. They argue that collaboration with the Nazi dictatorship called into question the Zionist establishment's dedication to the more significant Jewish cause and that it damaged the movement's moral authority in the eyes of many (Goldman, 1978).

Some academics were also concerned about the long-term impact of the Haavara Agreement on Jewish immigration to Palestine (Meyer, 1988; Porath, 1974). They claim that the agreement's peculiar circumstances permitted Nazi Germany to regulate who may move to Palestine, preferring persons with financial means and specific abilities (Ofer, 1990). This selection process, they argue, resulted in a more economically privileged Jewish community within Palestine, intensifying social and economic inequities and tensions within the growing Jewish population (Eldad, 1950; Wasserstein, 1979).

Furthermore, the Haavara Agreement has broader consequences for international Jewish solidarity and collaboration (Goldman, 1978). According to some researchers, the collaboration between Zionist leaders and Nazi officials during this period shattered the Jewish community's unity. They claim that the pact caused considerable differences and disagreements among Jewish groups, with some denouncing it for compromising with the Nazi dictatorship and others seeing it as a realistic method to preserve lives and assist Jewish resettlement (Morris, 1987). During and after World War II, the issues surrounding the pact continued to echo within Jewish communities, forming political and ideological differences.

Furthermore, some have highlighted concerns regarding the long-term impact of the Haavara Agreement on the relationship between Jews and Palestinians in Palestine (Pappé, 1992; Shlaim, 2000). They claim that the deal permitted the flow of finances and assets, accelerating Zionist settlement and land purchase in Palestine. This, in turn, fostered tensions and clashes between Jewish settlers and the indigenous Palestinian Arab population, foreshadowing the region's complex and volatile dynamics.

Overall, scholarly interpretations and criticisms of the Haavara Agreement illustrate the historical event's complexities. It is a contentious issue, with various perspectives providing valuable insights into the motivations, consequences, and ethical considerations surrounding the agreement and its impact on the Zionist movement, Jewish migration to Palestine, and the broader historical and political context. The wide diversity of viewpoints underlines the importance of further research and analysis to comprehend better this critical chapter in history (Sternhell, 1998; Brenner, 2007).

## References

1. Black, Edwin. The Transfer Agreement. 1991.

2. Brenner, Lenni. Zionism in the Age of the Dictators. 1983.

3. Caplan, Neil. Futile Diplomacy. 1970.

4. Cohen, Aharon. Israel and the Arab World. 1984.

5. Eldad, Israel. The Jewish Revolution. 1950.

6. Goldman, Nahum. The Jewish Paradox. 1978.

7. Hilberg, Raul. The Destruction of the European Jews. 1961.

8. Laqueur, Walter. A History of Zionism. 1972.

9. Meyer, Michael. Response to Modernity. 1988.

10. Morris, Benny. The Birth of the Palestinian Refugee Problem. 1987.

11. Nicosia, Francis. The Third Reich and the Palestine Question. 2008.

12. Ofer, Dalia. Escaping the Holocaust. 1990.

13. Pappé, Ilan. The Making of the Arab-Israeli Conflict. 1992.

14. Penslar, Derek. Zionism and Technocracy. 1991.

15. Porath, Yehoshua. The Emergence of the Palestinian-Arab National Movement. 1974.

16. Segev, Tom. The Seventh Million. 2000.

17. Shlaim, Avi. The Iron Wall. 2000.

18. Sternhell, Zeev. The Founding Myths of Israel. 1998.

19. Wasserstein, Bernard. Britain and the Jews of Europe. 1979.

# A Blood Alliance With the Devil

Here, we try to understand the complicated and varied relationship between Fascism and Zionism throughout the interwar period, shedding light on interesting case studies. These case studies offer intriguing insights into the ideological underpinnings, political connections, and far-reaching historical consequences of the union of these two complicated groups.

## 1) The Betar Movement

In 1923, Ze'ev Jabotinsky created the Betar Movement, envisioning a revisionist form of Zionism that underscored the paramount importance of establishing a Jewish state in Palestine (Shindler, 2014). Jabotinsky's connection with Fascism was indeed nuanced, influenced by the intellectual climate of the time, which witnessed the rise of authoritarian philosophies. Although Jabotinsky's association with certain aspects of Italian Fascism did not imply an endorsement of all its principles, he found merit in its emphasis on national strength, discipline, and organisational principles.

The Betar Movement was a Revisionist Zionist youth paramilitary organisation founded in 1923 in Riga, Latvia, by Vladimir (Ze'ev) Jabotinsky. It was one of several right-wing youth movements that arose at that
time and adopted special salutes and uniforms. The movement was characterised by physical training and paramilitary activities, which resonated
with certain facets of Fascist ideology (Heller, 2017).

Betar was active in smuggling illegal immigrants into Palestine from
Eastern Europe, especially from Poland, during the 1930s (Melzer). The
movement's long-term policy aimed at fighting Arab Palestinian resistance
to replace British colonialism with Jewish Zionism. It was just part of an
international Zionist movement with a colonial view of Palestine, although
it was planted even in China (Shichor, 2021). Betar's ideology originated in
a fusion of Vladimir Jabotinsky's "legionism" with the ideas of personal pioneering and defence exemplified in Joseph Trumpeldor's Life and Death
(Betar and Hadar).

The Betar Naval Academy, a Jewish naval training school, was founded
in 1934 in Civitavecchia, Italy by the Revisionist Zionist movement led
by Ze'ev Jabotinsky. Under Mussolini, the country was seen as a historical
reminder of the Jewish people's beginnings and a modern example of a
once-glorious culture recovering its role in the world via the affirmation of
power and national pride.

The aggressive nature of the Betar Movement, characterised by physical
training and paramilitary activities, resonated with certain facets of Fascist
ideology. The terrorism it exercised on the Palestinian locals tells tons
about the roots of the movement and its ideology. Jabotinsky's admiration
for specific elements of Fascism stemmed from his unwavering belief in
the significance of a robust Jewish national identity and the imperative of
self-defence in the face of mounting Arab opposition in Palestine (Medoff,
1994). He conceived of the "new Jew" as assertive, self-reliant, and capable
of safeguarding Jewish interests—a concept reminiscent of Fascist notions
regarding a regimented and armed society. Nevertheless, it is crucial to
underline that Jabotinsky was a staunch opponent of Fascist anti-Semitism
and a fervent defender of Jewish rights.

## 2) The Irgun

The Irgun, a paramilitary organisation led by Menachem Begin, played a pivotal role in the struggle for Jewish dominance in Palestine (Bell, 1996). Employing armed terrorism against both British and Arab rule, the Irgun was profoundly influenced by the tenets of Revisionist Zionism, which sought to reclaim the entirety of historic Palestine during the interwar period.

Begin regarded Jabotinsky as a mentor and drew inspiration from his militant style. While the Irgun did establish contacts with Fascist Italy and Nazi Germany, some authors think it worth emphasising that these interactions were driven by practical considerations rather than ideological alignment (Schechtman, 1956). Maybe there was no alignment on all the lines, but there was indeed ideologic affinity, without which no business could be done. Moreover, the terrorism practised by these first Zionist movements against the British and Arabs is enough evidence that they were, at the core, fascist – terrorism that did not stop even after the creation of their state and its recognition by their Western allies. Just look at the map of Palestine and how it changed from 1946 to this day (GEW Editorial, 2023). All the same, these changes were not made by peaceful means but by genocides.

The goal was to garner support for Jewish immigration and the establishment of a Jewish state, even if it cost the Zionist movement to sign with blood an infamous alliance with the devil. With several engagements with Fascist Italy, Begin and the Irgun could not remain unstained in their commitment to Jewish self-determination. The basis upon which the Jewish state was built will remain tainted forever with their alliance with Fascism. Nothing could erase this original sin. You cannot act as an agent of the devil and pretend that your actions were motivated by a deep-seated desire to ensure the survival and prosperity of your people. That makes you and your people both at the service of the demon.

The history of Israel, staked with bloodbaths, is evidence highlighting the substantial gap between the so-called pragmatic approach of the Irgun and its actual adherence to Fascist ideology.

## 3)The Haavara (Transfer) Agreement

Inked in 1933 by Zionist leaders and Nazi Germany, authorised the transfer of Jewish assets from Germany to Palestine. This agreement is another piece of evidence to be added to the case of Zionist affinities with Fascism and Nazism. However, some authors would find a way to pretend that it was driven by pragmatic considerations (Black, 2001). Its objectives encompassed the preservation of Jewish wealth amidst Nazi-controlled Germany, the facilitation of Jewish immigration to Palestine, and the support of a Jewish state's establishment (Nicosia, 1985). Zionist leaders viewed this pact as an opportunity to rescue Jewish lives and resources, even if it necessitated collaboration with an anti-Semitic regime. However, it is imperative to acknowledge that the Haavara Agreement represented a complex and divisive episode in Zionist history, with numerous Zionist groups and individuals vehemently opposing it.

Zionist leaders spearheaded the negotiations of the Haavara Agreement, like Chaim Weizmann and the Jewish Agency, prompted by the dire circumstances faced by German Jews amid escalating Nazi persecution. Recognising the importance of safeguarding Jewish assets and facilitating Jewish immigration, they decided to engage with Nazi authorities on critical economic matters. This collaboration shows to what extent they would obtain what they wanted: a portion of land in the Middle East called for thousands of years Palestine.

## 4) Palestine

The term "Palestine" has multiple possible etymologies. One possible origin is the Late Bronze Age when Palestine was commonly used (Nur, 2016). Another possible etymology is rooted in the demystification of states and the crisis of representation in the social sciences and humanities, leading to Palestine's recent admissibility as a legitimate ethnographic subject (Furani, Rabinowitz, 2011). The name Palestine is also found in Greek texts from the mid-fifth century B.C., suggesting another potential origin (Jacobson, 1999). Furthermore, the concept of Palestine as a coherent geo-political unit dates back to 3000 B.C., according to both Palestinian and Zionist narratives (Pappe, 2008). Lastly, the upheavals of the seventh century C.E. uprooted the Christian idea of Palestine as a land of inheritance (Wilken, 1988).

The term "Palestine" originally originated in the 5th century BCE, when Herodotus, an ancient Greek historian, wrote about a "region of Syria called Palaistinê." The English term "Palestine" comes from the Latin Palaestna, which comes from the Koine Greek v, Palaistn, which Herodotus used. From the beginning of the twentieth century, Palestinians utilised the phrase to self-identify (Feldman, 1990).

The name "Palestine" is usually thought to have originated from the land of the Philistines, but this may not be the case. The term is thought to be derived from the Egyptian and Hebrew words "peleshet," which means rolling or migrating. The Philistines (Kirk, 2023) were the country's inhabitants to the northeast of Egypt who used this word.

During the Mutasarrifate of Jerusalem (under the Ottoman Empire), the term "Palestine" became prevalent in Early Modern English and was used in both English and Arabic. The British also used it to refer to "Mandatory Palestine," an area from the former Ottoman Empire partitioned in the Sykes-Picot Agreement and secured by Britain through the League of Nations' Mandate for Palestine.

The first traces of the name Palestine come from the time of Ramses II and III, roughly around the mid-12th century BC. An inscription dated to around 1150 BC at the Medinet Habu temple in Luxor refers to the Peleset (PLST) among those who fought against Ramses III. Today, we know the Peleset as the Philistines (Masalha, 2020).

Palestinians' modern national identity has its roots in nationalist discourses that evolved among the peoples of the Ottoman Empire in the late
nineteenth century and were heightened following the creation of modern
nation-state boundaries in the Middle East during World War I.

## 5) The Colonial Ambitions of Fascist Italy

Under Benito Mussolini's leadership, Fascist Italy had territorial ambitions in Africa, particularly Libya and Ethiopia. Their colonial ambitions
occasionally collided with the goals of the Zionist movement, particularly
when Zionist leaders sought coalitions to promote Jewish immigration
and obtain support for forming a Jewish state (Tal, 1997). It is critical to
realize that such relationships were motivated by strategic factors rather
than shared ideological ideals.

With the British Mandate's restricted immigration policy and mounting Arab opposition, Zionist leaders sought new ways to facilitate Jewish
immigration and gain international support. In other cases, they considered allying with Fascist Italy, which had geographical overlap in North
Africa and similar regional goals. On the other hand, these contacts were
strictly transactional (Rodogno, 2006). Zionist leaders recognized that
the foundation of a Jewish state was their primary goal, and they sought
relationships based on geopolitical calculations rather than shared ideals.

We acquire a more comprehensive grasp of the complicated relationships between Fascism and Zionism throughout the interwar period by
analyzing these case studies. It is critical to approach this complicated
subject subtly, acknowledging that interactions occurred within a larger
political and historical framework (Hertzberg, 2013; Steinweis, 2009). We
can traverse the complexity and paradoxes during this crucial moment in
Jewish history by examining these examples.

# References

1. Bell, J. B. Terror Out of Zion. 1996.

2. Betar and Hadar." □□□□□□□□'□ □□□□Page. Accessed November 5, 2023. https://en.jabotinsky.org/zeev-jabotinsky/life-story/betar-and-hadar/.

3. Black, Edwin. The Transfer Agreement. 2001.

4. FELDMAN, LOUIS H. "Some Observations on the Name of Palestine." Hebrew Union College Annual 61 (1990): 1–23. http://www.jstor.org/stable/23508170.

5. Furani, Khaled. Dan, Rabinowitz. (2011). The Ethnographic Arriving of Palestine. Annual Review of Anthropology, Available from: 10.1146/ANNUREV-ANTHRO-081309-145910

6. GEW Editorial. (2023). "A Land Without People for a People Without Land"! - GEW Reports & Analyses. Last modified October 16, 2023. https://g-ew.com/2023/10/a-land-without-people-for-a-people-without-land/.

7. Heller, Daniel Kupfert, 'Little Fascists?', Jabotinsky's Children: Polish Jews and the Rise of Right-Wing Zionism (Princeton, NJ, 2017; online ed, Princeton Scholarship Online, 24 May 2018), https://doi.org/10.23943/princeton/9780691174754.003.0003, accessed 16 Nov. 2023.

8. Herf, Jeffrey. Nazi Propaganda for the Arab World. 2009.

9. Hertzberg, Arthur. The Zionist Idea. 2013.

10. Jacobson, David, M. (1999). Palestine and Israel. Bulletin of the American Schools of Oriental Research, doi: 10.2307/1357617

11. Khalidi, Rashid. The Iron Cage. 2006.

12. Kirk, Gabi. "Commodifying Indigeneity? Settler Colonialism and Racial Capitalism in Fair Trade Farming in Palestine", Historical Materialism 31, 2 (2023): 236-268, doi: https://doi.org/10.116 3/1569206x-bja10013

13. Laqueur, Walter. A History of Zionism. 1972.

14. Medoff, Rafael. Militant Zionism in America. 1994.

15. Masalha, Nur. (2016). The Concept of Palestine: The Conception Of Palestine from the Late Bronze Age to the Modern Period. doi: 10.3366/HLPS.2016.0140

16. Melzer, Emanuel. "Betar." The YIVO Encyclopedia of Jews in Eastern Europe. Accessed November 5, 2023. https://yivoency clopedia.org/article.aspx/Betar.

17. Nicosia, Francis R. The Third Reich and the Palestine Question. 1985.

18. Pappe, Ilan. (2008). The One Palestine: Past, Present and Future Perspectives.

19. Rodogno, Davide. Fascism's European Empire. 2006.

20. Schechtman, Joseph. Fighter and Prophet: The Vladimir Jabotinsky Story. 1956.

21. Shindler, Colin. The Rise of the Israeli Right. 2014.

22. Shichor, Yitzhak. "Betar China: The Impact of a Remote Jewish Youth Movement, 1929-1949." Jerusalem Center for Public Affairs. Last modified August 19, 2021. https://jcpa.org/article/betar-china-the-impact-of-a-remote-jewish-youth-movement-1929-1949/.

23. Steinweis, Alan E. Studying the Jew. 2009.

24. Tal, David. War in Palestine, 1948. 1997.

25. "The Right To Resist - GEW Reports and Analyses." GEW Reports & Analyses. Last modified October 25, 2023. https://g-ew.com/2023/10/the-western-civilisation-is-losing-its-soul/.

26. Wilken, Robert, L. (1988). Byzantine Palestine: A Christian Holy Land. The Biblical archaeologist, doi: 10.2307/3210073

# ETHICAL AND MORAL IMPLICATIONS

The Haavara Agreement is often justified on grounds of pragmatism, given the dire circumstances Jews faced in Nazi Germany (Brenner, 2007). This chapter discusses the moral dilemma that Zionist leaders faced: the immediate rescue of Jews against the long-term consequences of collaborating with the Nazis (Laqueur, 2003).

The Haavara (Transfer) Agreement and its links to Mussolini and Revisionist Zionism present severe ethical and moral issues (Cohen, 1984; Porat, 1986). This chapter goes into the intricacies of these consequences. It gives a more in-depth review of the various perspectives and arguments.

One of the critical difficulties in considering the ethical implications of the Haavara Agreement is the concept of collaboration with and support for a morally repugnant state such as Nazi Germany (Black, 2001; Nicosia, 1985). According to critics, by joining an agreement that facilitated the transfer of Jewish assets to Germany, the Zionist movement indirectly supported and collaborated with the Nazi regime. They argue that cooperation with the Nazis legitimised their acts and policies, no matter how well-meaning.

This raises significant concerns about the limitations of pragmatism and morality in the face of adversity. Some say that when German Jews faced increased persecution and the possibility of extermination, any action that could save lives and alleviate the suffering of those caught in the Nazi regime's web was morally and ethically significant (Brenner, 2007). They emphasise the major hurdles and complex moral arithmetic confronted by Zionist leaders who were forced to make life-or-death decisions, evaluating the worth of immediate rescue against the potential long-term implications of cooperating with the Nazis.

Furthermore, some opponents say that the Haavara Agreement hampered the broader boycott and economic isolation of the Nazi regime (Penslar, 1991). They argue that the Agreement damaged the international consensus against Hitler's government by compromising with Nazi Germany and promoting their trade. By allowing Germany to import critical items from Palestine, the Nazis could transfer resources towards their military building and expansionist aspirations, contributing to the Holocaust's continuance (Segev, 2000).

On the other hand, proponents of the Haavara Agreement emphasise the grave circumstances that German Jews were in at the time. They claim that the deal saved the lives of Jews fleeing persecution and allowed them to save part of their assets before fleeing. They contend that the ethical imperative of saving lives and assisting people in need surpassed the moral quandary of cooperating with Nazi Germany (Friling, 2005; Aharoni, 1984). Furthermore, they emphasise that the Haavara Agreement permitted the emigration of around 60,000 German Jews to Palestine, which helped to establish and develop the future Jewish state. However, they omit to say that those who benefited from cooperating with the Nazis have been selected among the ablest in terms of finance and wealth. It was the elite of the Jewish people. The others have been left to die. The argument obviously undermines the ethical purpose of saving the Jews from the Holocaust. Thus, the basis of Israel was founded on lies and immoral means, which is quite normal for a colonisation movement ready to take a country by force and kill whoever opposes its project. Ultimately, this means that the state of Israel has been built on an agreement between Nazis and Fascists, Zionist leaders included. The price was the latter's acceptance of the Holocaust – whose victims were mostly the poor – in return for the freedom of selected Jews.

Studying the more considerable historical background is critical to fully comprehend the Haavara Agreement's ethical implications. The world community, mainly Western nations, generally ignored the misery of German Jews in the 1930s. Strict immigration limits and stringent rules made it extremely difficult for Jews to flee to other countries. Jewish leaders believed the pact with Nazi Germany provided a flawed but practical way of helping them progress with their Zionist project (Dwork, 1991; Wyman, 1984).

Another crucial ethical consideration is the involvement of the World Zionist Organisation and its leaders, who thought they were "forced" to make tough decisions under extreme duress (Elon, 1975; Vital, 1999). They were tasked with striking a difficult balance between saving selected Jewish lives, which undermines any moral integrity of the Zionist movement, and joining the resistance against Hitler and Mussolini. They chose the first option. As a result, their decisions have substantial unethical ramifications and pose critical questions about the obligations and difficulties of crisis leadership.

Mussolini's collaboration with Revisionist Zionism has moral ramifications that must be carefully considered (Pinto, 1998). The Fascist administration of Mussolini was infamous for its repressive policies and anti-Semitism. The question is whether Revisionist Zionists like Ze'ev Jabotinsky compromised their moral ideals by seeking assistance from a ruler with such a tainted reputation (Zimmerman, 1999). This prompts thought about the complexities of political alliances and the ethical quandary of aligning oneself with morally flawed leaders to achieve strategic aims. While some argue that the alliance with Mussolini was a pragmatic choice to obtain support for the Zionist cause, others reject any relationship with an evil tyrant.

The ethical implications of the Haavara Agreement, as well as its linkages to Mussolini and Revisionist Zionism, must be examined with nuance and respect. Individual and organisational decisions taken during this turbulent period should be evaluated in the historical context of the time (Laqueur, 2003; Wasserstein, 1996). The complexities of these ethical and moral consequences highlight the difficult choices that must be made in the face of tremendous adversity. We can better understand the ethical quandaries and obstacles in negotiating ethically complicated situations by investigating their implications.

## References

1. Aharoni, Ada. The Second Exodus. 1984.

2. Black, Edwin. The Transfer Agreement. 2001.

3. Brenner, Lenni. Zionism in the Age of Dictators. 2007.

4. Cohen, Michael J. Zionism and Arabism in Palestine and Israel. 1984.

5. Dwork, Deborah. Flight from the Reich. 1991.

6. Elon, Amos. The Israelis: Founders and Sons. 1975.

7. Friling, Tuvia. Arrows in the Dark. 2005.

8. Laqueur, Walter. A History of Zionism. 2003.

9. Nicosia, Francis R. The Third Reich and the Palestine Question. 1985.

10. Penslar, Derek. Zionism and Technocracy. 1991.

11. Pinto, Diana. Israel Has Moved. 1998.

12. Porat, Dina. The Blue and the Yellow Stars of David. 1986.

13. Segev, Tom. The Seventh Million. 2000.

14. Vital, David. A People Apart. 1999.

15. Wasserstein, Bernard. Israel and Palestine. 1996.

16. Wyman, David S. Paper Walls. 1984.

17. Zimmerman, David. The Italian Encounter with Tudor England. 1999.

# CONCLUSION

The Zionist project, from the outset, was not meant to be a secular democratic state where Jews, Christians and Muslims would be living together in peace. It was meant to be what we see right now: An apartheid, military-led state with hegemonic views on all the Middle East region, from the Nile to the Euphrates. That's why on 14 February 1896, in Leipzig and Vienna, when an Austrian Jewish journalist called Theodor Herzl published his most renowned book, he gave it the title Der Judenstaat (The Jewish State). Herzl was not interested in democracy and secularism, not even in Judaism. He analysed the causes of anti-Semitism in this pamphlet and recommended the establishment of a Jewish state as a solution. He envisioned establishing a future independent Jewish state in the twentieth century and pushed Jews to buy land in Palestine. The book is regarded as one of the most important texts of modern Zionism, which was built on a lie: that the land – Palestine – was empty and waiting for the Zionists to come and populate it. The lie made the expropriation of the local owners a violent procedure that necessitated the Jewish Zionist settlers to do precisely what the European white men did in America and Australia: one genocide after another until no more people were claiming Palestine as their motherland.

Later on, pursuing the same goal described by Hertzl, the Zionist leaders will not shy away from any obstacle to achieve what they believed to be a right or a duty, or maybe both, including cooperation with the worst enemy of the Jewish people.

The state of Israel has been possible thanks to an arrangement - known as the Haavara Agreement - between the Zionist leaders and the Nazi and Fascist regimes during the second world war. The proponents of the Haavara Agreement emphasised the grave circumstances that German Jews were in at the time. They claimed that the deal saved the lives of Jews fleeing persecution and allowed them to save part of their assets before fleeing. They contend that the ethical imperative of saving lives and assisting people in need surpassed the moral quandary of cooperating with Nazi Germany. Furthermore, they emphasise that the Haavara Agreement permitted the emigration of around 60,000 German Jews to Palestine, which helped to establish and develop the future Jewish state. However, they omit to say that those who benefited from this cooperation with the Nazis have been selected among the ablest in terms of finance, wealth, education and social capital (which further explains why Israel was much more scientifically and technologically advanced than all its neighbours, apart from the help it received from the USA and its allies). The elite of the Jewish people had been saved for the future state. The others have been left to die in the gas chambers.

This historical fact undermines the ethical purpose of saving the Jews from the Holocaust. Thus, the basis of Israel was founded on lies and immoral means, which does not contrast with the immorality of a colonisation movement ready to take a country by force and kill whoever opposes its project. In the end, this also implies that behind the image of the "only democracy in the Middle East," there are not only thousands of Arab Palestinian victims who have been displaced, expelled, or killed but also millions of Jews who the Zionist leaders forsook to the Nazis. The establishment of a Zionist state on someone else's land came with the unspoken acknowledgement of the Holocaust in exchange for the liberation of certain Jews.

Finally, the investigation of the historical and intellectual relationship between Fascism and Zionism provides valuable insights into the complexities of this topic. We have discussed the Haavara Agreement, Mussolini's attitude towards revisionist Zionism, and the ideological distinctions and similarities between these two forces in previous chapters.

The Haavara Agreement, which authorised the transfer of Jewish capital and assets to Palestine, facilitated Jewish immigration and settlement. Despite being contentious and met with opposition from both Zionist and anti-Zionist elements, the pact revealed a transitory confluence of interests between Fascist Italy and the Zionist movement. This one-of-a-kind collaboration was motivated by political expediency and a shared commitment to address the deteriorating predicament of European Jews and their ambition for a homeland.

The investigation of Mussolini's position on revisionist Zionism revealed a strange and somewhat confusing scenario. While publicly condemning portions of Judaism and openly expressing anti-Semitic attitudes, Mussolini was nonetheless fascinated by the Zionist cause. His admiration for Jews' perseverance and nationalist aspirations resulted in a strange relationship distinguished by tolerance and encouragement.

Mussolini's backing for Zionism stemmed partly from his idea that Jews constituted a distinct racial and national entity. This viewpoint varied from the common anti-Semitic ideas of his period, which saw Jews as a threat to racial purity. Fascism, as an authoritarian ideology based on the exaltation of the nation-state, found common ground with the Zionist movement's pursuit of a Jewish homeland. Mussolini's acknowledgement of Jewish nationalism could be interpreted as an attempt to exploit this passion for the benefit of his government while strengthening his views of nation-building.

The ideological differences and similarities between Fascism and Zionism revealed varied perspectives. Fascism advocated a nationalistic and authoritarian ideology that intended to unite the Italian people under the protection of a powerful state: Mussolini's Italy prized order, discipline, and the fascist goal of national renewal. Zionism, on the other hand, was motivated by a desire to maintain and strengthen Jewish identity. While their techniques differed significantly, both movements supported nationalism. They attempted to revitalise a feeling of identity in their communities.

It is vital to stress that Jewish support for Fascism was not uniform or universal. Due to the perceived dangers posed by authoritarian ideologies, many Jews, particularly those emphasising their devotion to their own countries, resisted collaboration with Fascist regimes. Nonetheless, amid Europe's difficult position during the interwar period, some individuals, motivated by the need to defend their society, made pragmatic decisions to cooperate with Fascist regimes.

Scholarly interpretations and criticisms have defined our knowledge of this complex relationship. While some scholars suggest that this confluence of interests should be understood as a pragmatic alliance based on mutual convenience, others contend that Fascism and Zionism had a true ideological affinity. Scholars disagree over how much Mussolini's admiration for Zionism influenced his policy. Furthermore, continued research and analysis of sources shed new light on the actions and intentions of those involved in this intricate connection.

Throughout the case studies analysed, we watched several occurrences that shed light on the varied character of the Fascism-Zionism relationship. From individual Jews joining Fascist organisations to Mussolini's diplomatic manoeuvrings in the international arena, these incidents highlight the complicated interplay of ideas, politics, and actions. It is critical to recognise that these incidents did not occur in isolation but as part of larger historical contexts moulded by geopolitical interests, socio-cultural dynamics, and the changing condition of Jews in Europe.

Furthermore, the investigation of the Fascism-Zionism relationship should not be conducted in isolation. However, it should consider the broader historical context of the interwar period. During this period, the growth of Fascism in Europe was distinguished by a complex interplay of authoritarianism, nationalism, anti-Semitism, and the search for identity amid political and economic turbulence. The Zionist movement arose against this backdrop, aiming to alleviate the continuous prejudice and persecution of Jews while pursuing a sense of national identity.

Finally, investigating this historical link poses significant ethical and moral issues. Analysing the relationship between Fascism and Zionism forces us to address the tough decisions made by Jews during a period of tremendous persecution and prejudice. It also challenges us to consider the consequences of allying with an authoritarian regime for self-preservation. The ethical implications of the Haavara Agreement, for example, continue to spark debate about the challenges faced by Zionist leaders who attempted to rescue Jews while cooperating with a fascist administration.

In summary, the connection between Fascism and Zionism is a complex mix of historical events, different beliefs, and ethical dilemmas. This research thoroughly examined this intricate link, highlighting the need for ongoing scholarly research and critical discussion. By exploring the different aspects of this connection, we better understand the past and the challenges of dealing with issues of identity, survival, and cooperation during difficult times. It serves as a reminder that history is never straightforward and that the interplay of beliefs, politics, and personal decisions can have complex and occasionally unexpected effects on events.

# BIBLIOGRAPHY

1. Aharoni, Ada. 1984. The Second Exodus. Dorrance Pub Co.

2. Anderson, Benedict.1983. Imagined Communities: Reflections on the Origin and Spread of Nationalism. Verso.

3. Auerbach, J. 2009. The Zionist Ideology. University Press of New England.

4. Avineri, Shlomo. 1981. The Making of Modern Zionism: Intellectual Origins of the Jewish State." Basic Books.

5. Bell, J. B. 2017. Terror Out of Zion. Routledge.

6. Black, Edwin. "The Transfer Agreement: The Dramatic Story of the Pact Between the Third Reich and Jewish Palestine." Carroll & Graf, 1984.

7. Bosworth, R. J. B. Mussolini. Bloomsbury Publishing, 2002.

8. Brenner, Lenni. Zionism in the Age of the Dictators. Lawrence Hill & Co., 1983.

9. Breuilly, John. Nationalism and the State*. Manchester: Man-

chester University Press, 1982.

10. Caplan, Neil. Futile Diplomacy. 1970.

11. Ciano, G. (2000). "Ciano's Diplomatic Papers". Odhams.

12. Cohen, Aharon. Israel and the Arab World. 1984.

13. Cohen, Michael J. Zionism and Arabism in Palestine and Israel. 1984.

14. Cohen, M. J. (1987). "Zion and State: Nation, Class and the Shaping of Modern Israel". Wiley.

15. De Felice, R. (1998). "Mussolini: The Jews and the Laws of Race". Antenore.

16. Dowty, Alan. Closed Borders: The Contemporary Assault on Freedom of Movement. Yale University Press, 1987.

17. Dwork, Deborah. Flight from the Reich. 1991.

18. Eatwell, Roger. *Fascism: A History*. New York: Allen Lane, 1995.

19. Eldad, Israel. The Jewish Revolution. 1950.

20. Elon, Amos. The Israelis: Founders and Sons. 1975.

21. Evans, Richard J. "The Coming of the Third Reich." Penguin Group, 2003.

22. Evans, Richard J. "The Third Reich in Power." Penguin Group, 2005.

23. Friling, Tuvia. Arrows in the Dark. 2005.

24. Goldman, Nahum. The Jewish Paradox. 1978.

25. Griffin, Roger. *The Nature of Fascism*. New York: St. Martin's Press, 1991.

26. Heller, Joseph. The Birth of Israel, 1945–1949: Ben-Gurion and His Critics. University Press of Florida, 2000.

27. Herf, Jeffrey. Nazi Propaganda for the Arab World. 2009.

28. Herf, Jeffrey. Nazi Propaganda for the Arab World. Yale University Press, 2009.

29. Hertzberg, A. (1979). "Zionism: A Political History". Palgrave Macmillan.

30. Hertzberg, Arthur. The Zionist Idea. 2013.

31. Hertzberg, Arthur. *The Zionist Idea: A Historical Analysis and Reader*. Jewish Publication Society, 1997.

32. Herzog, Hanna. "Gendering Politics: Women in Israel." University of Michigan Press, 1999.

33. Hilberg, Raul. The Destruction of the European Jews. 1961.

34. Kershaw, Ian. *Hitler: A Biography*. New York: W. W. Norton & Company, 2008.

35. Kershaw, Ian. "Hitler: A Biography." W. W. Norton & Company, 2008.

36. Khalidi, Rashid. The Iron Cage. 2006.

37. Khalidi, Rashid. "The Iron Cage: The Story of the Palestinian Struggle for Statehood." Beacon Press, 2007.

38. Kitchen, M. (1996). "Europe Between the Wars". Longman.

39. Laqueur, W. (2003). "A History of Zionism". Tauris Parke Paperbacks.

40. Laqueur, Walter. A History of Zionism. 1972.

41. Laqueur, Walter. A History of Zionism. 1972.

42. Laqueur, Walter. A History of Zionism. 2003.

43. Laqueur, Walter. "A History of Zionism." Holt, Rinehart and Winston, 1972.

44. Laqueur, Walter. *A History of Zionism*. New York: Schocken Books, 2003.

45. Laqueur, Walter. "A History of Zionism." Tauris Parke Paperbacks, 2003.

46. Laqueur, Walter. A History of Zionism. Tauris Parke Paperbacks, 2003.

47. Laqueur, Walter. "Zionism and Fascism." *Middle Eastern Studies* 7, no. 2 (1971): 163–178.

48. Laqueur, W. & Rubin, B. (2001). "The Israel-Arab Reader". Penguin.

49. Medoff, Rafael. Militant Zionism in America. 1994.

50. Meyer, Michael. Response to Modernity. 1988.

51. Morris, B. (1999). "Righteous Victims: A History of the Zionist-Arab Conflict, 1881-1999". Knopf.

52. Morris, Benny. "Righteous Victims: A History of the Zion-

ist-Arab Conflict, 1881-2001." Vintage, 2001.

53. Morris, Benny. The Birth of the Palestinian Refugee Problem. 1987.

54. Nicosia, Francis R. The Third Reich and the Palestine Question. 1985.

55. Nicosia, Francis R. The Third Reich and the Palestine Question. 1985.

56. Nicosia, Francis R. "The Third Reich and the Palestine Question." University of Texas Press, 1985.

57. Nicosia, Francis R. "Zionism and Anti-Semitism in Nazi Germany." *Cambridge University Press*, 2008.

58. Nicosia, Francis R. "Zionism and Anti-Semitism in Nazi Germany." Cambridge University Press, 2008.

59. Nicosia, Francis R. Zionism and Anti-Semitism in Nazi Germany. Cambridge University Press, 2008.

60. Nicosia, Francis. The Third Reich and the Palestine Question. 2008.

61. Ofer, Dalia. Escaping the Holocaust. 1990.

62. Pappé, Ilan. The Making of the Arab-Israeli Conflict. 1992.

63. Paxton, R. O. (2004). "The Anatomy of Fascism". Knopf.

64. Paxton, Robert O. "The Anatomy of Fascism." Knopf, 2004.

65. Paxton, Robert O. The Anatomy of Fascism. Knopf, 2004.

66. Paxton, Robert O. *The Anatomy of Fascism*. New York: Alfred

A. Knopf, 2004.

67. Payne, Stanley G. "A History of Fascism, 1914–1945." UCL Press, 1995.

68. Penslar, D. (2007). "Zionism and Technocracy: The Engineering of Jewish Settlement in Palestine, 1870-1918". Indiana University Press.

69. Penslar, D. (2011). "Israel in History". Routledge.

70. Penslar, Derek. Zionism and Technocracy. 1991.

71. Penslar, Derek. Zionism and Technocracy. 1991.

72. Penslar, Derek. *Zionism and Technocracy: The Engineering of Jewish Settlement in Palestine, 1870–1918*. Indiana University Press, 1991.

73. Pini, G. (2008). "Mussolini and the Middle East, 1933-1938". Middle Eastern Studies, 44(5), 715-734.

74. Pini, G. (2008). "Mussolini and Zionism: A Re-examination of Fascist Policy Toward the Jews". Middle Eastern Studies, 44(3), 435-454.

75. Pinto, Diana. Israel Has Moved. 1998.

76. Porat, Dina. The Blue and the Yellow Stars of David. 1986.

77. Porath, Yehoshua. The Emergence of the Palestinian-Arab National Movement. 1974.

78. Rabinovich, I. (2004). "The Yom Kippur War: The Epic Encounter That Transformed the Middle East". Schocken.

79. Rodogno, Davide. Fascism's European Empire. 2006.

80. Rose, Paul Lawrence. *Revolutionary Zionism: The Ideological Development of Ze'ev Jabotinsky*. Cambridge University Press, 2010.

81. Salvatorelli, L. M. (1957). "Mussolini and the Origins of the Second World War". Praeger.

82. Schechtman, J. B. (1986). "The Jabotinsky Saga". Gefen Publishing House.

83. Schechtman, Joseph B. "The Vladimir Jabotinsky Story: Rebel and Statesman." Thomas Yoseloff, 1956.

84. Schechtman, Joseph. Fighter and Prophet: The Vladimir Jabotinsky Story. 1956.

85. Segev, Tom. "One Palestine, Complete: Jews and Arabs Under the British Mandate." Little, Brown, 2000.

86. Segev, Tom. The Seventh Million. 2000.

87. Segev, Tom. The Seventh Million. 2000.

88. Shindler, C. (2002). "The Land Beyond Promise: Israel, Likud and the Zionist Dream". I.B. Tauris.

89. Shindler, Colin. *Jabotinsky: A Life*. Yale University Press, 2014.

90. Shindler, Colin. The Rise of the Israeli Right. 2014.

91. Shindler, Colin. "The Rise of the Israeli Right: From Odessa to Hebron." Cambridge University Press, 2015.

92. Shlaim, Avi. The Iron Wall. 2000.

93. Smith, Anthony D. "National Identity and the Idea of European Unity." *International Affairs* 68, no. 1 (1992): 55–76.

94. Smith, Anthony D. National Identity. University of Nevada Press, 1991.

95. Smith, D. (1997). "Mussolini: A Biography". Vintage.

96. Sorek, T. (2007). "Arab Soccer in a Jewish State: The Integrative Enclave". Cambridge University Press.

97. Steinweis, Alan E. Studying the Jew. 2009.

98. Sternhell, Zeev. "Fascist Ideology." In *Fascism: A Reader's Guide*, edited by Walter Laqueur, 315–376. Berkeley: University of California Press, 1976.

99. Sternhell, Zeev. *The Birth of Fascist Ideology*. Princeton University Press, 1994.

100. Sternhell, Zeev. The Founding Myths of Israel. 1998.

101. Sznajder, Mario, and Luis Roniger. *The Legacy of Human Rights Violations in the Southern Cone*. Oxford: Oxford University Press, 1999.

102. Tal, David. War in Palestine, 1948. 1997.

103. Tomes, J. (2001). "Mussolini and Italian Fascism". Nelson Thornes.

104. Tuccille, J. (1971). "It Usually Begins With Ayn Rand". Stein and Day.

105. Vital, D. (1999). "The Origins of Zionism". Clarendon Press.

106. Vital, D. (2000). "A People Apart: The Jews in Europe, 1789-1939". Oxford University Press.

107. Vital, David. A People Apart. 1999.

108. Vital, David. *The Origins of Zionism*. Oxford: Clarendon Press, 1975.

109. Wasserstein, Bernard. Britain and the Jews of Europe. 1979.

110. Wasserstein, Bernard. Israel and Palestine. 1996.

111. Waxman, Dov. "The Ideological Foundations of the Boycott Movement against Israel." Digest of Middle East Studies, vol. 22, no. 1, 2013, pp. 36–56.

112. Whitman, James Q. *Hitler's American Model: The United States and the Making of Nazi Race Law*. Princeton University Press, 2017.

113. Wyman, David S. Paper Walls. 1984.

114. Zimmerman D. (2003). "Contested Memories: Poles and Jews During the Holocaust and Its Aftermath". Rutgers University Press.

115. Zimmerman, David. The Italian Encounter with Tudor England. 1999.

116. Zweig, R. W. (1981). "The Gold Train: The Destruction of the Jews and the Looting of Hungary". Harper.

# Book Two: Part (11): Jews Against Israel

# GREAT MINDS AND ANTI-ZIONIST JEWS

## (1) Key Differences Between Zionism and Anti-Zionism

Zionism and anti-Zionism are two opposing ideologies that have played significant roles in defining the Middle East's political environment, particularly concerning the Israeli-Palestinian conflict.

## Definition and Goals

Zionism is a political movement that emerged in the 19th century in Europe, intending to establish a Jewish homeland in the Middle East. This movement used both anti-Semitism and Western imperialist objectives in the Middle East to create a "safe haven for Jews" by dispossessing the Palestinians from their land. With the assistance of the United States and some of its Western allies, the Zionist movement resulted in the foundation of the modern state of Israel in 1948.

Anti-Zionism, on the other hand, opposes the establishment and support of a Jewish state in the Middle East. Anti-Zionists argue that the creation of Israel as a Jewish state has led to the displacement and oppression of the Palestinian people. Some anti-Zionists view Zionism as a colonial-settler project that was only achievable through an alliance with colonial powers.

## Critiques and Opposition

Critiques of Zionism often focus on its impact on the Palestinian people. Critics argue that the establishment of a Jewish state in Palestine has led to the displacement of Palestinians, the appropriation of their land, and the denial of their right to self-determination.

Some argue that anti-Zionism is a form of anti-Semitism, as it denies the Jewish people's right to self-determination. But this is an empty argument, as evidenced by the fact that many Jews, previously mentioned, are anti-Zionists and accusing them of anti-Semitism is just nonsense.

Both Zionism and anti-Zionism have had a substantial impact on the Israeli-Palestinian conflict. Zionism culminated in the establishment of the state of Israel, which has been at the centre of the conflict.

Anti-Zionism, on the other hand, has fueled opposition to the state of Israel and support for Palestinian rights.

However, many people don't know that some prominent Jews, like Einstein, Freud, Arendt, Asimov, Chomsky, etc., are anti-Zionist.

## (2) Most Jews Do Not Live In Israel

The Jews who oppose Israel are predominantly ultra-Orthodox anti-Zionist organisations, the most prominent of which is Neturei Karta (NK). NK, founded in 1938, opposes the modern state of Israel because it believes that the Jewish people do not have the right to self-determination and that only God can restore Jewish sovereignty in the land of Israel by introducing the Messiah. NK has a considerable following in the United States and regards itself as the religious Jewish authority on Zionism and Israel. They wish for the peaceful demise of the state of Israel.

NK's views do not represent the majority of the Jewish community. While the ultra-Orthodox community largely disapproves of Israel's secular government and liberal policies, the vast majority thoroughly abhors and rejects Neturei Karta's ideology. But NK are not the only Jews that oppose Israel.

Satmar Hasidism is another anti-Zionist movement. They see Zionism and the foundation of the State of Israel as anti-messianic acts born of sin. They believe that the Jewish people were commanded not to use physical force to return to the Land of Israel, nor to "rebel against the nations of the world," nor to "hasten the End." They were compelled to wait for heavenly, complete, miraculous, supernatural, and meta-historical salvation that is different from human striving.

It is important to note, first, that "most Jews do not live in Israel". On the other hand, not all Jews hold these views. According to a Pew Research Centre survey, 45% of US Jewish adults say that caring about Israel is "essential" to what it means to be Jewish. The survey, however, discovered that Jewish Americans have significantly disparate views on Israel and its political leadership.

## (3) Anti-Zionism and Anti-Semitism

Anti-Semitism and anti-Zionism, while sometimes conflated, are distinct concepts. Anti-Semitism refers to hostility and prejudice directed against Jewish people, based on age-old stereotypes and myths that target Jews as a people, their religious practices and beliefs, or the Jewish State of Israel. Anti-Zionism, on the other hand, is opposed to the political movement of Zionism, which advocates for the establishment and support of a Jewish state in Palestine. This land is wholly Arabised and Islamised for centuries.

Jewish – like Arab and Muslim- anti-Zionism expresses resistance against a political movement used by imperialist powers to control the

Middle East after the end of the XXth century colonialism. It has nothing to do with anti-Semitism. The evidence is that many Jewish people are still living in Arab Muslim countries, as they used to for centuries, safe and secure. Only in Europe have the Jews been harmed. Hence, their unfortunate flight to Palestine where mobilised by Zionism, they did not try to integrate into the life of the locals but preferred to have their own state at the expense of the Palestinians. Then, they became more greedy and started making their way by the force of weapons, aided by the same Western imperialist powers.

The Working Definition of Anti-semitism of the International Holocaust Remembrance Alliance acknowledges explicitly that criticism of Israel, while comparable to critiques directed at any other nation, should not be seen as an expression of antisemitism.

Anti-Zionism has nothing to do with anti-Semitism. Some Jewish groups, such as the Satmar Hasidic sect or Neturei Karta (NK) oppose the state of Israel on religious grounds, believing that an actual Jewish state can only be established with the coming of the Messiah.

In conclusion, anti-Zionism and anti-Semitism are not the same. Anti-Semitism is a form of prejudice against Jews, while anti-Zionism is opposition to the political ideology of Zionism. It's crucial to distinguish between legitimate criticism of Israeli policies and anti-Semitic rhetoric or actions.

## (4) Some of the greatest Jewish minds are anti-Zionists.

Several prominent Jewish figures have opposed Zionism or refused to serve Israel. These individuals come from various fields, including academia, literature, and the arts. Here are some notable examples:

**Albert Einstein**: The renowned physicist was a vocal critic of the idea of an ethnically exclusive Israeli state.

**Karl Marx**: The author of "The Capital" and "The Jewish Question"...

**Sigmund Freud:** The founder of psychoanalysis, believed that the claim of Zionist Jews to the Land of Israel could not be a realistic political claim.

**Primo Levi:** The writer and Auschwitz survivor compared the plight of Palestinians to that of Jews.

**Isaac Asimov:** The famous science fiction writer stated that he was not a Zionist and criticised the idea of any heritage being considered more important than others.

**Hannah Arendt:** The political theorist criticised Zionism for its reliance on antisemitism.

**Noam Chomsky:** The linguist and philosopher has been a vocal critic of Israeli policies and has questioned the rationality behind the state's creation.

**Richard Falk:** The former UN special rapporteur on human rights in the Occupied Palestinian Territories has called Israeli policies in the Occupied Territories "a crime against humanity".

**Haredi Jews:** Since the founding of the State of Israel in 1948, Haredi Jews have refused to serve in the Israeli military for religious reasons.

**Yaakov Meiersohn and Joseph Berger**: Members of the Jewish-Marxist Poale Zion, they turned into anti-Zionists in the early 1920s after realising that Zionism would be discriminatory.

**International Jewish Anti-Zionist Network:** This is a secular, socialist, antiwar, anti-imperialist organisation that calls for "the dismantling of Israeli apartheid, return of Palestinian refugees, and the ending of the Israeli colonisation of historic Palestine".

**George Steiner, Tony Judt, and Baruch Kimmerling**: These intellectuals of Jewish background in Israel and the diaspora have been noted for their anti-Zionist or post-Zionist views.

**Rabbi Joel Teitelbaum:** The founding Satmar Rebbe was one of the most prominent anti-Zionists of the twentieth century, who formulated a detailed theological rationale for his opposition to the state of Israel.

And many others...

# (5) Why Jewish Intellectuals Oppose Zionism?

Jewish intellectuals who oppose Zionism do so for a variety of reasons, including religious beliefs and interpretations, political and ethical concerns, critique of Israeli policies, support for Palestinian rights, and opposition to nationalism and ethnic exclusivity.

**Religious Beliefs and Interpretations:** Some Orthodox Jews oppose Zionism on religious grounds, viewing the creation of a Jewish state as preempting the Messiah. They believe that the return to the land of Israel and the creation of a state should be divine acts, not human ones. They also object to the secular nature of Zionism, which they see as using sacred terms like "Zion", "Jerusalem", "Land of Israel", "redemption" and "ingathering of exiles" in a secular and literal sense, rather than as sacred terms.

**Political and Ethical Concerns**: Some Jewish intellectuals oppose Zionism because they see it as a threat to efforts to facilitate Jewish citizenship and equality within the European nation-state context. They argue that Zionism espouses nationalism in a secular fashion, which they see as problematic. Some also view Zionism as a form of nationalism, which they claim to be a product of capitalist societies.

**Critique of Israeli Policies**: Some Jewish intellectuals critique Zionism due to their opposition to certain policies of the State of Israel. They argue that these policies violate human rights and international law. This critique is often linked to a broader critique of imperialism and colonialism, with Zionism seen as a representation of Western power.

**Support for Palestinian Rights**: Some Jewish intellectuals oppose Zionism due to their support for Palestinian rights. They contend that the Palestinians were forcibly removed from their homeland upon the establishment of the State of Israel. They see this as a form of colonial dispossession and argue for the rights of Palestinians to self-determination and sovereignty.

**Opposition to Nationalism and Ethnic Exclusivity**: Some Jewish intellectuals oppose Zionism because they see it as promoting nationalism and ethnic exclusivity. They say that a state should not be based on a single racial or religious identity. Instead, there should be a civic nation where every citizen has the same rights and duties, no matter what racial or religious group they belong to.

# (6) Historical Events That Influenced Jewish Anti-Zionist Views

Several historical occurrences and ideological shifts have influenced Jewish anti-Zionist views. Here are some key events and movements that have shaped these views:

**Orthodox Jewish Opposition to Zionism**: Orthodox Jewish communities have historically opposed Zionism, viewing it as a secular movement that undermines the religious nature of Judaism. They believe that the establishment of a Jewish state should only occur through divine intervention, not human action. This belief is rooted in the Talmudic oaths that prohibit Jews from establishing a state by force and rebelling against the nations of the world. The Neturei Karta is a well-known group that holds these views.

**Political Zionism's emergence in the late 19th century**: Orthodox Jews, contending that only the Messiah could re-establish Jewish rule in Israel, opposed it on religious grounds. Secular Jews also opposed it, uncomfortable with the idea that Jewish peoplehood was a national or ethnic identity.

**Rise of Nationalism in Europe**: The rise of nationalism in Europe in the late 19th and early 20th centuries influenced Jewish anti-Zionist views. Some Jews saw Zionism as a form of nationalism, which they opposed as a product of capitalist societies. They also saw it as a threat to their acceptance and integration in the countries where they resided.

**Arab Christian and Palestinian Anti-Zionist Movements**: Palestinian Christians and Arab nationalists have also influenced Jewish anti-Zionist views. Palestinian Christians have been active in promoting Palestinian nationalism and resisting Zionism. Conversely, Arab nationalists have regarded Zionism as a potential menace to their ambitions, particularly with the growth of the Zionist labour movement and its "Hebrew labour" programme.

**Antisemitism and Anti-Zionism**: Antisemitism has also played a role in shaping Jewish anti-Zionist views. Some Jews have opposed Zionism because they believe it fuels antisemitism by promoting a distinct Jewish national identity. They argue that this undermines the acceptance and integration of Jews in the countries where they reside.

These historical events and movements have shaped Jewish anti-Zionist views in complex ways, reflecting a range of religious, political, and social perspectives.

# References and Further Reading

## (1) Key Differences Between Zionism and Anti-Zionism

[1] https://www.bbc.com/news/magazine-36160928

[2] https://www.britannica.com/topic/Zionism

[3] https://www.jstor.org/stable/2537506

[4] https://www.adl.org/resources/blog/anti-zionism-antisemitism-how-anti-zionist-language-left-and-right-vilifies-jews

[5] https://www.aljazeera.com/opinions/2012/12/24/zionism-anti-semitism-and-colonialism

[6] https://www.jstor.org/stable/2535480

[7] https://www.ajc.org/sites/default/files/pdf/2020-10/AntiZionism%20and%20Antisemitism.pdf

[8] https://www.brookings.edu/articles/how-do-americans-feel-about-zionism-antisemitism-and-israel/

[9] https://www.jewishvirtuallibrary.org/anti-semitism-and-anti-zionism

[10] https://www.jstor.org/stable/23563220

[11] https://www.adl.org/resources/tools-and-strategies/what-anti-isr ael-anti-semitic-anti-zionist

[12] https://www.jewishvirtuallibrary.org/a-definition-of-zionism

[13]https://www.cambridge.org/core/books/cambridge-history-of-jud aism/zionism-and-its-critics/73C4F39C05491B593F680206CAB87978

[14] https://www.jstor.org/stable/23529420

[15] https://www.adl.org/resources/backgrounder/anti-zionism

[16] https://www.adl.org/resources/backgrounder/zionism

[17] https://www.historystudies.net/dergi/tar201512085fc.pdf

[18] https://www.intelligencesquared.com/events/anti-zionism-is-ant i-semitism/

[19] https://www.theguardian.com/news/2019/mar/07/debunking -myth-that-anti-zionism-is-antisemitic

[20] https://www.vox.com/2018/11/20/18080010/zionism-israel-pal estine

[21] https://www.aljazeera.com/opinions/2019/1/9/the-zionist-fallac y-of-jewish-supremacy

[22] https://www.newyorker.com/news/q-and-a/is-anti-zionism-anti -semitism

[23] https://georgetownvoice.com/2023/03/24/anti-zionism-and-ant isemitism-are-not-the-same/

[24] https://www.heyalma.com/israel-guide/what-is-zionism/

## (2) Most Jews Do Not Live In Israel

[1] https://www.adl.org/resources/backgrounder/neturei-karta

[2] https://www.jewishvirtuallibrary.org/anti-zionism-among-jews

[3] https://www.pewresearch.org/short-reads/2021/05/21/u-s-jews -have-widely-differing-views-on-israel/

[4] https://www.myjewishlearning.com/article/ultra-orthodox-anti-zi

onist/

[5] https://www.annefrank.org/en/topics/antisemitism/are-all-jews-zionists/

[6] https://www.pewresearch.org/religion/2021/05/11/u-s-jews-connections-with-and-attitudes-toward-israel/

## (3) Anti-Zionism and Anti-Semitism

[1] https://www.ajc.org/sites/default/files/pdf/2020-10/AntiZionism%20and%20Antisemitism.pdf

[2] https://www.bbc.com/news/magazine-36160928

[3] https://www.adl.org/resources/blog/anti-zionism-antisemitism-how-anti-zionist-language-left-and-right-vilifies-jews

[4] https://www.adl.org/resources/tools-and-strategies/what-anti-israel-anti-semitic-anti-zionist

[5] https://www.theguardian.com/news/2019/mar/07/debunking-myth-that-anti-zionism-is-antisemitic

[6] https://www.newyorker.com/news/q-and-a/is-anti-zionism-anti-semitism

[7] https://www.jewishvirtuallibrary.org/anti-semitism-and-anti-zionism

[8] https://www.wsj.com/articles/anti-zionism-is-a-more-malevolent-form-of-anti-semitism-jews-israel-hamas-b84c59de

## (4) Prominent Anti-Zionist Jews

[1] https://www.stopwar.org.uk/article/from-albert-einstein-to-noam-chomsky-famous-jews-who-have-opposed-israel/

[2] https://katz.sas.upenn.edu/resources/blog/most-anti-zionist-text

[3] https://www.adl.org/resources/blog/roger-waters-extends-his-lega cy-antisemitic-rhetoric

[4] https://www.jewishvirtuallibrary.org/anti-zionism-among-jews

[5] http://ieg-ego.eu/grillt-2011-en

[6] https://forward.com/opinion/430535/a-lot-more-jews-are-anti-zi onists-than-you-think/

[7] https://www.smithsonianmag.com/history/one-hundred-years-ag o-einstein-was-given-heros-welcome-americas-jews-180977386/

[8] https://www.jewishvoiceforpeace.org/member-stories/

[9] https://katz.sas.upenn.edu/taxonomy/term/424

[10] https://www.scientificamerican.com/article/how-2-pro-nazi-nob elists-attacked-einstein-s-jewish-science-excerpt1/

[11] https://www.jewishnashville.org/our-impact/community-relatio ns/community-relations-committee/roger-waters-spreads-hate

[12] https://www.jstor.org/stable/2535683

[                1                    3                    ] https://www.haaretz.com/jewish/2015-11-23/ty-article/what-was-einste ins-relationship-to-judaism-and-zionism/0000017f-f443-d497-a1ff-f6c3 77e30000

[                1                    4                    ] https://www.haaretz.com/israel-news/2018-11-20/ty-article/.premium/i sraeli-professors-warn-against-equating-anti-zionism-with-anti-semitism/ 0000017f-dc1e-d856-a37f-fdded13e0000

[15] https://www.theguardian.com/news/2019/mar/07/debunking -myth-that-anti-zionism-is-antisemitic

[16] https://press.princeton.edu/books/hardcover/9780691144122/e instein-before-israel

[17] https://www.wsj.com/articles/anti-zionism-is-a-more-malevolent -form-of-anti-semitism-jews-israel-hamas-b84c59de

[18] https://arabcenterdc.org/resource/is-anti-zionism-a-form-of-anti -semitism/

[19] https://www.vanderbilt.edu/AnS/physics/brau/H182/Term%20 Papers/Eric%20Weiss.html

## (5) Why Jewish Intellectuals Oppose Zionism?

[1] https://www.britannica.com/topic/fundamentalism/Jewish-fund amentalism-in-Israel

[2] https://www.jstor.org/stable/10.5325/jjewiethi.4.2.0109

[                          3                          ] https://www.haaretz.com/israel-news/2021-04-15/ty-article-opinion/.pr emium/between-antisemitism-and-anti-zionism-the-intellectuals-dilemm a/0000017f-db54-d3ff-a7ff-fbf495350000

[4] https://www.adl.org/resources/report/antisemitism-and-radical-a nti-israel-bias-political-left-europe

[5] https://www.jstor.org/stable/29779843

[6] https://www.jewishvirtuallibrary.org/anti-zionism-among-jews

[7] https://academic.oup.com/book/9169/chapter/155801542

[8] https://academic.oup.com/book/39979/chapter/340295066

[                          9                          ] https://georgetown.edu/welcome/student_news/detail?_kgoui_bookma rk=e3637e94-03e0-5062-8b5b-f2e05174defa&feed=student_news_1&i d=085d42bf-813c-5df0-b1d2-0034dadad3f0

[10] https://academic.oup.com/book/628/chapter/135333910

[11] https://www.theguardian.com/news/2019/mar/07/dcbunking -myth-that-anti-zionism-is-antisemitic

[12] https://www.jstor.org/stable/4467521

[13]https://publishing.cdlib.org/ucpressebooks/viewanchor.id=d0e27 18&brand=eschol&chunk.id=s1.3.6&doc.view=content&docId=ft709n b49x&toc.depth=100

[14] https://merip.org/2022/10/changing-attitudes-towards-zionism -among-american-jews-an-interview-with-zachary-lockman/

[15] https://criticallegalthinking.com/2018/08/27/against-appeasem ent-whats-wrong-with-zionism/

[16] https://www.jstor.org/stable/2535683

[17] https://www.adl.org/resources/blog/anti-zionism-antisemitism
-how-anti-zionist-language-left-and-right-vilifies-jews

[18] https://arabcenterdc.org/resource/is-anti-zionism-a-form-of-anti
-semitism/

[19] https://www.loc.gov/rr/amed/pdf/palestine4/Is-Zionism-the-sol
ution-of-the-Jewish-problem.pdf

## (6) Historical Events That Influenced Jewish Anti-Zionist Views

[1] https://www.jewishvirtuallibrary.org/anti-zionism-among-jews

[2] https://www.jstor.org/stable/30245608

[3] https://digitalcommons.georgiasouthern.edu/cgi/viewcontent.cgi
?article=1122&context=aujh

[4] https://muse.jhu.edu/article/239325/pdf

[5] https://www.fpri.org/article/2015/01/origins-and-evolution-of-zi
onism/

[6] https://www.jstor.org/stable/40213810

[7] http://ieg-ego.eu/grillt-2011-en

[8] https://www.britannica.com/topic/political-Zionism

[9] https://lsa.umich.edu/content/dam/cmenas-assets/cmenas-docu
ments/unit-of-israel-palestine/Section1_Zionism.pdf

[10] https://www.adl.org/resources/blog/anti-zionism-antisemitism
-how-anti-zionist-language-left-and-right-vilifies-jews

[11] https://www.myjewishlearning.com/article/ultra-orthodox-anti
-zionist/

[12] https://www.britannica.com/topic/Zionism

[13]https://www2.rivier.edu/faculty/lcarr/Some%20thoughts%20on
%20the%20relationships%20between%20nationalism,%20anti-Zionism%
20and%20anti-Semitism..pdf

[14] https://www.un.org/unispal/historical-timeline/

[16] https://www.nli.org.il/en/discover/israel/zionism/zionism-history

[17] https://www.aljazeera.com/opinions/2019/1/9/the-zionist-fallac
y-of-jewish-supremacy

[18] https://encyclopedia.ushmm.org/content/en/article/antisemitis
m-in-history-the-era-of-nationalism-1800-1918

[19] https://www.adl.org/resources/backgrounder/neturei-karta

[20] https://academic.oup.com/book/628/chapter/135334068

[21] https://www.adl.org/resources/report/antisemitism-and-radical
-anti-israel-bias-political-left-europe

# Book Three:
# Resisting Zionist
# Colonisation

# CONCEPTUAL FRAMEWORK

## Definition of Key Terms:

1. Colonialism: The act of one nation asserting control over another territory, often involving the displacement of indigenous populations and the exploitation of resources (Loomba, 1998; Said, 1993).

2. Imperialism: An extension of a country's power and influence through diplomacy or military force, often linked with economic exploitation (Hobson, 1902; Nkrumah, 1965).

3. Zionism: A political ideology and movement that advocates for establishing a Jewish homeland, primarily in what was once Palestine and is now called Israel (Herzl, 1896; Shlaim, 2000).

4. Islamism: There is not one definition, but several. Some suggest it is a political ideology that seeks to implement Islamic law and principles in governance and may involve various strategies, including democratic participation, activism, or armed struggle (Roy, 1994; Esposito, 2000). But initially, it was an intellectual and reformist movement that started

in the 19th century in the Arab world, led by Gamal al-Dine al-Afghani, Mohamed Abdu, and Rashid Ridha in Egypt. It is called Nahdha (Awakening in the sense of Renaissance). It called for the Islamic Union to face the European challenge that came with Napoleon's conquest of Egypt. It represented the first anti-colonialist call to confront Europe and stop the imperialist wave.

## Theoretical Foundations:

1. Anti-colonialism: Theories and practises that oppose colonial rule, often advocating for the liberation of colonised peoples and territories (Fanon, 1961; Memmi, 1965).

2. Liberation Theory: A body of thought arguing for the liberation of marginalised groups from various forms of oppression, often drawing from Marxist and critical theory frameworks (Freire, 1970; Hooks, 1984).

3. Islamic Political Thought: This is a broad term for the different Islamic ideas and practises that deal with government, social justice, and statehood. These ideas and practises can be similar to or different from Western political theories (Qutb, 1964; Soroush, 1998).

## Introduction

To fully comprehend the complexities of the subject matter, it is essential to establish a strong conceptual framework. This chapter aims to provide a comprehensive understanding of the critical concepts and theories that underpin the analysis of political Zionism as a segment of global imperialism(Smith, 2016). By exploring these foundational principles, we can delve deeper into the historical, political, and social dynamics surrounding the Zionist movement(Anderson, 2015).

## Defining Political Zionism:

Political Zionism, as a concept, refers to the ideology and movement that emerged in the late 19th century intending to establish a Jewish homeland in Palestine (Herzl, 1896). It originated as a response to the growing anti-Semitism Jews faced in various parts of the world, particularly in Europe (Pinsker, 1882). Establishing a sovereign Jewish state became the primary objective of political Zionism, leading to the formation of the Zionist Organisation and subsequent efforts to secure international support for this endeavour (Laqueur, 1972).

## Imperialism and its Relationship to Political Zionism:

Imperialism involves complex economic, political, and cultural dynamics by which dominant powers exert influence and control over weaker nations or territories (Hobson, 1902). The relationship between political Zionism and imperialism is multifaceted (Said, 1979). While some argue that political Zionism can be viewed as a form of settler colonialism and imperialism (Veracini, 2010), others suggest that it can be understood as a response to and a product of existing imperialist structures (Shlaim, 2000).

To further understand the connection between political Zionism and imperialism, examining the imperialist context of the late 19th and early 20th centuries is crucial. The dominance of European colonial powers during this period significantly impacted the aspirations and strategies of the Zionist movement.

European imperial powers, such as Britain, France, and Germany, sought to secure their geopolitical interests in the Middle East and Africa, primarily driven by economic motivations and geopolitical power games. The strategic location of Palestine and its potential as a gateway to the region's vast resources made it a coveted prize for these imperial powers.

Key events, such as the Sykes-Picot Agreement of 1916, which divided up the Middle East between Britain and France, and the subsequent Balfour Declaration of 1917, demonstrate the convergence of political interests between the Zionist movement and imperial powers (Khalidi, 2010). The Balfour Declaration, in particular, expressed Britain's support for the establishment of a Jewish homeland in Palestine, providing crucial international recognition and backing for the Zionist cause.

## Global Power Dynamics:

Understanding the global power dynamics at play during the emergence and growth of political Zionism is crucial (Chomsky, 1999). The dominance of European colonial powers during this period profoundly impacted the aspirations and strategies of the Zionist movement. For example, the Balfour Declaration of 1917 exemplifies the convergence of political interests between the Zionist movement and imperial powers seeking to secure their own geopolitical objectives (Fromkin, 1989).

Additionally, the rise of nationalist movements worldwide during this period created a fertile environment for political Zionism to gain traction. The desire for self-determination and decolonisation among various communities laid the groundwork for the Zionist movement to present itself as a legitimate national liberation movement seeking a homeland for a historically oppressed group. This adept positioning enabled political Zionism to resonate with the broader global context of anti-colonial struggles.

## Nationalism and Identity:

Political Zionism is deeply rooted in nationalism and identity formation (Smith, 1991). The movement sought to revive a collective Jewish identity and forge a sense of national belonging by establishing a Jewish state. The interplay between nationalistic aspirations, religious sentiments, and the enduring Jewish diaspora played a significant role in shaping the conceptual framework of political Zionism.

At its core, political Zionism aimed to redefine the Jewish people as a national group with collective rights and aspirations rather than solely a religious community. Leaders such as Theodor Herzl saw political sovereignty as essential for overcoming the challenges faced by Jewish communities in Europe and elsewhere (Herzl, 1896), ranging from discrimination and persecution to lingering effects of the diaspora. This transformative ideology sought to unite Jews from diverse backgrounds, with different cultural practises and languages, under a collective national identity (Zerubavel, 1995).

## Critical Perspectives:

Examining political Zionism through critical lenses is essential (Finkelstein, 2003) to fully comprehend its implications and consequences. Scholars have raised important questions regarding the rights of indigenous Palestinian communities, the justifiability of displacing them in favour of Jewish settlers, and the broader implications of such actions on regional stability and peace.

Critics argue that political Zionism, often framed as a liberation movement, can be seen as a form of settler colonialism that perpetuated the dispossession and subjugation of the Palestinian people (Pappé, 2006). They point to the forced displacement, human rights violations, and ongoing conflicts that emerged as a result of the establishment of Israel. These critical perspectives challenge the narrative of political Zionism as a purely emancipatory movement, forcing a closer examination of the complexities and power dynamics involved.

## Conclusion:

Establishing a robust conceptual framework is essential to grasp the complexities of political Zionism (Smith, 2016). In understanding its roots, interactions with global imperialism, and the underlying dynamics of nationalism and identity, we can navigate the subsequent chapters' analysis with a clear understanding of the forces at play. By critically evaluating and questioning these foundational principles, we can lay the groundwork for a comprehensive examination of political Zionism's historical context, tactics, and the resistance it engendered (Said, 2003). This extended conceptual framework allows for a nuanced exploration of the multiple perspectives and contentious issues that surround the topic, ultimately enriching our understanding of political Zionism as a facet of global imperialism.

## References

1. Anderson, Benedict. "Imagined Communities: Reflections on the Origin and Spread of Nationalism." Verso, 2015.

2. Chomsky, Noam. "Fateful Triangle: The United States, Israel, and the Palestinians." South End Press, 1999.

3. Esposito J. L. (2000). *Islamic Threat: Myth or Reality?* Oxford University Press.

4. Fanon F. (1961). *The Wretched of the Earth*. Grove Press.

5. Freire P. (1970). *Pedagogy of the Oppressed*. Herder and Herder.

6. Finkelstein, Norman. "Image and Reality of the Israel-Palestine Conflict." Verso, 2003.

7. Fromkin, David. "A Peace to End All Peace: The Fall of the Ottoman Empire and the Creation of the Modern Middle East." Holt, 1989. Herzl, Theodor. "Der Judenstaat." 1896.

8. Herzl T. (1896). *The Jewish State*. Dover Publications.

9. Hobson J. A. (1902). *Imperialism: A Study*. James Pott & Co.

10. Hooks b. (1984). *Feminist Theory: From Margin to Center*. South End Press.

11. Khalidi, Rashid. "The Iron Cage: The Story of the Palestinian Struggle for Statehood." Beacon Press, 2010.

12. Laqueur, Walter. "A History of Zionism." Holt, Rinehart and Wilson, 1972.

13. Loomba A. (1998). *Colonialism/Postcolonialism*. Routledge.

14. Memmi A. (1965). *The Colonizer and the Colonized*. Orion Press.

15. Nkrumah K. (1965). *Neo-Colonialism: The Last Stage of Imperialism*. Thomas Nelson & Sons.

16. Pappé, Ilan. "The Ethnic Cleansing of Palestine." One World, 2006.

17. Pinsker, Leon. "Auto-Emancipation." 1882.

18. Qutb S. (1964). *Milestones*. Dar al-Ilm.

19. Roy O. (1994). *The Failure of Political Islam*. Harvard University Press.

20. Said, Edward. "Orientalism." Pantheon, 1979.

21. Said, Edward. "Culture and Imperialism." Knopf, 2003.

22. Shlaim A. (2000). *The Iron Wall: Israel and the Arab World*. W. W. Norton & Company.

23. Soroush A. (1998). *Reason, Freedom, and Democracy in Islam. Oxford University Press.

24. Smith, Anthony D. "National Identity." University of Nevada Press, 1991.

25. Smith, Tony. "Why Wilson Matters: The Origin of American Liberal Internationalism and Its Crisis Today." Princeton University Press, 2016.

26. Veracini, Lorenzo. "Settler Colonialism: A Theoretical Overview." Palgrave Macmillan, 2010.

27. Zerubavel, Yael. "Recovered Roots: Collective Memory and the Making of Israeli National Tradition." University of Chicago Press, 1995.

# Zionist Cloning of European Colonialism in Palestine

Zionism originated from a controversial affair. It resulted from European antisemitism, which triggered the Jewish desire for freedom, and Western imperialism, seeking to exert control in the Middle East. This occurred while the Arabs aimed for liberation and unity. The Zionist endeavour was driven by the interests of Western imperialism and the power aspirations of the Jewish secular elite, which later evolved into greed and military expansion. Consequently, the Zionist project was never intended to create a peaceful coexistence for Jews and Arabs on the same land; instead, it was designed as a war machine serving fascist ideals. This was particularly relevant given the rise of fascism before World War One.

"Zionism" encapsulates a profound political ideology and consequential movement during the latter half of the 19th century. This movement ardently aspired to forge a Jewish homeland within the historical region of

Palestine. Emerging from the depths of religious and nationalist fervour, the political ideology of Zionism began to flourish, propelled by the pressing need to counter the alarming surge of anti-Semitism that plagued the European continent (Hertzberg, 2004). The Zionist cause, which sought to establish a homeland for the Jewish people, owes much of its success to the influential figures who championed its ideals. Among these luminaries, Theodor Herzl stands out as a pivotal figure whose unwavering dedication galvanised support and paved the way for the eventual realisation of the State of Israel in 1948.

Herzl possessed an acute understanding of the political landscape and the pressing need for a Jewish homeland. Herzl articulated a compelling argument for establishing a sovereign Jewish nation through his seminal work, "The Jewish State," published in 1896. His persuasive rhetoric resonated deeply with Jews worldwide, igniting a fervour to shape history. Herzl's tireless efforts extended beyond the realm of literature. He skillfully navigated diplomatic circles, engaging with influential figures and world leaders to garner support for the Zionist cause. His diplomatic prowess was displayed during the First Zionist Congress in Basel, Switzerland, in 1897. This historic gathering brought together Jewish representatives from across the globe, united in their shared aspiration for a homeland they had to create piece by piece, for it was nowhere on earth yet. A homeland for the Jews of the world who were unhappy in their countries! For this, they needed to dispossess other people from their land to make their homeland. It was a crazy idea! But it's not so crazy, given that colonial powers have already done the same dirty job. So, it was to those same colonial powers that Zionists pleaded their cause. The matter was "simple": "We just want to clone your colonial experience in Palestine"! That was a lovely song ringing in the ears of European colonialists. Zionism has nothing against colonial Europe. It just sought to be a good student.

Understanding political Zionism requires exploring its historical background. This involves examining the significant migration of Jewish communities to Palestine in the early 20th century.

This influx of individuals seeking refuge and a sense of belonging was accompanied by the active involvement of the British authorities in fostering the aspirations of the Zionist movement, as evidenced by the influential Balfour Declaration. The repercussions of these developments have reverberated throughout the region, engendering a series of protracted conflicts that continue to exert a profound influence on the geopolitical landscape today (Morris, 2008). The phenomenon of Jewish communities embarking on a meaningful journey towards the land of Palestine finds its roots in the latter half of the 19th century, an epoch commonly referred to as the First Aliyah. The surge of immigration witnessed during this period can be attributed to a confluence of factors, encompassing the escalating tide of anti-Semitism sweeping across Europe, the rise of fervent nationalist movements, and the yearning for a Jewish homeland (Morris, 2008).

The discernible manifestation of the British involvement in fostering Zionist ambitions materialised through the issuance of the Balfour Imperialist Declaration in 1917. The fact that he promised land that he did not own to the Zionists, who had no right to possess it, did bother the British Minister.

The infamous proclamation, bearing the name of the British Foreign Secretary, Arthur Balfour, resolutely conveyed an unwavering endorsement for the inception of a "national abode" dedicated to the Jewish populace within the territorial confines of Palestine. Thus, Israel's history started with a rape, in which Britain was an accomplice.

The British approach, as observed by scholars, was perceived as a calculated manoeuvre aimed at cultivating goodwill among influential Jewish communities across Europe and the United States, with the ultimate objective of garnering their support during the tumultuous period of World War I (Anderson, 2013). This war also witnessed Britain's betrayal of its Arab allies (Sherif Hussein and his sons), as the British failed to keep their promises to the Arabs, who helped them defeat the Ottoman Empire.

The historic Balfour Declaration, an ill-famed document reverberating across the geopolitical landscape, catalysed the subsequent British mandate over the region of Palestine. This portentous declaration, issued by the British government in 1917, not only solidified the aspirations of the

Zionist movement but also propelled it towards greater prominence on the global stage.

The intricate tapestry of regional conflicts indelibly marked the region's geopolitical landscape is inextricably linked to the enduring Israeli-Palestinian conundrum. In the wake of the establishment of the State of Israel in 1948, a contentious debate unfolded among neighbouring Arab countries and the indigenous Palestinian population, questioning the legitimacy of this nascent state (Morris, 2008). The historical trajectory of the region has been marked by a succession of armed conflicts and strategic manoeuvres, notably including the 1948 Arab-Israeli War, the Six-Day War in 1967, and the Yom Kippur War in 1973. The protracted and tumultuous conflicts that unfolded in the region have regrettably led to the displacement of many Palestinians, numbering in the hundreds of thousands. This regrettable consequence has further exacerbated the deep-rooted grievances and animosities between the Israeli and Palestinian factions.

Moreover, this literary masterpiece endeavours to shed light upon the intricate interplay between the tenets of political Zionism and the far-reaching tendrils of global imperialism. Through a meticulous analysis of the geopolitical inclinations of prominent global players and their entanglement with the Zionist movement, a compelling narrative emerges, underscoring the strategic calculus behind the inception of the State of Israel. It becomes apparent that this momentous development was, in fact, a calculated manoeuvre by imperial powers to uphold their dominion and wield their influence within the intricate tapestry of the Middle East (Khalidi, 2007). In their relentless endeavour to safeguard their imperial pursuits, the British discerned a propitious opening by supporting Zionist aspirations, garnering favour with influential Jewish communities across Europe and the United States (Anderson, 2013). The convergence of interests paved the way for the flourishing and subsequent acquisition of political influence by the Zionist movement in Palestine.

The multifaceted nature of political Zionism necessitates a comprehensive examination of its occupation tactics, which have undeniably left a profound impact. The intricate tapestry of the Israeli-Palestinian conflict is woven with the threads of displacement, colonisation, and the denial of fundamental human rights. From the annals of history, one cannot overlook the profound impact of the Zionist endeavour, which has left an indelible mark on the Palestinian landscape. As elucidated by renowned historian Ilan Pappe in his seminal work, the systematic colonisation of Palestinian land and the establishment of Israeli settlements in occupied territories are pillars of the Zionist project (Pappe, 2006). This multi-faceted saga unfolds with a complexity that demands our attention and scrutiny. In its pursuit of regional dominance and control, the Israeli government has deftly employed a multifaceted array of strategies. These tactics encompass the erection of a formidable separation wall, imposing stringent permits and checkpoints, and implementing discriminatory laws that significantly impact the everyday existence of Palestinians (Kimmerling & Migdal, 2003). Implementing these strategies has led to the disintegration of Palestinian land, impeding the creation of a sustainable Palestinian nation and jeopardising the prospects for an equitable and enduring resolution.

In conclusion, it is imperative to delve into the steadfast opposition that has arisen against the phenomenon of Zionist colonialism throughout the annals of history. In a remarkable display of resilience and determination, the Palestinian people, in collaboration with their steadfast allies, have valiantly risen against the myriad injustices imposed upon them. From the grassroots level to the realm of armed resistance, their unwavering struggle for justice and liberation has reverberated across the region (Halper, 2018). The global landscape has witnessed a notable surge in the prominence of nonviolent demonstrations, exemplified by the Boycott, Divestment, and Sanctions (BDS) movement, which has garnered significant support on an international scale. This movement, rooted in the pursuit of justice for the Palestinian people, has emerged as a formidable tool to challenge Israeli policies and advocate for the rights of Palestinians (Morrison, 2021). Armed resistance has emerged as a formidable response in the face of occupation, particularly in heightened conflict. Notably, groups such as Hamas and the Popular Front for the Liberation of Palestine (PFLP) have actively engaged in armed struggle against Israeli forces (Rubenberg, 2010). The indomitable spirit and unwavering resolve exhibited by those advocating for the Palestinian cause are a constant source of inspiration, igniting a fervour of international solidarity campaigns.

## References:

1. Anderson, B. (2013). The Zionist project and British imperial policy in Palestine, 1917-1929. Israel Studies, 18(2), 1-24.

2. Halper, J. (2018). War against the people: Israel, the Palestinians and global pacification. Pluto Press.

3. Hertzberg, A. (2004). The Zionist idea: A historical analysis and reader. Jewish Publication Society.

4. Khalidi, R. (2007). The Iron Cage: The story of the Palestinian struggle for statehood. Beacon Press.

5. Kimmerling, B., & Migdal, J. S. (2003). The Palestinian People: A history. Harvard University Press.

6. Morris, B. (2008). The birth of the Palestinian refugee problem revisited. Cambridge University Press.

7. Morrison, D. (2021). BDS: Boycott, Divestment, Sanctions: The global struggle for Palestinian rights. Haymarket Books.

8. Pappe, I. (2006). The ethnic cleansing of Palestine. Oneworld

Publications.

9. Rubenberg, C. (2010). Israeli politics and the Palestinian Minority. Lynne Rienner Publishers.

# THE WORLD IS UPSIDE DOWN! WEST LOST SOUL!

Historical backdrop, political ideology, and religious convictions have all affected the Palestinian resistance against the Zionist occupation of Palestine. The historical context includes events such as the establishment of the State of Israel in 1948 and the subsequent exodus of Palestinians (Zaki, 2020). This historical wrong has inspired Palestinian resistance and resolve to reclaim their rights and sovereignty.

Political beliefs have also had a significant impact on the Palestinian resistance. In response to Zionism and the foundation of a Jewish state in Palestine, Palestinian nationalism arose (Zaki, 2020). Various ideologies, including secular nationalism, socialism, and Islamism, have impacted the Palestinian national movement. Founded in 1964, the Palestinian Liberation Organisation (PLO) initially supported a secular nationalist ideology and intended to construct a secular democratic state in Palestine (Hejazi, 2020). However, the development of Islamist parties such as Hamas has given the Palestinian conflict a spiritual dimension (Faeq, Jahnata, 2020).

In the late 1980s, Hamas, an offshoot of the Muslim Brotherhood, formed a resistance movement and has since blended religious and nationalist aspirations (Faeq, Jahnata, 2020; Abdelhakam, 2020).

Religious convictions, as in other national liberation movements (previously in Algeria, Tunisia, Morocco, Sudan, Egypt, and so on), have greatly affected the Palestinian struggle against Zionism. As Palestinians' primary religion, Islam has given a cultural and ideological underpinning for resistance (Hejazi, 2020). Palestinians see their battle as defending their land and resisting occupation, and they use religious narratives and symbols to rally support (Hejazi, 2020). Many Palestinians have responded positively to religious speech and the absorption of Islamic ideals within the Palestinian national struggle, contributing to their perseverance in the face of adversity.

In their fight against French and British imperialism, Arab nationalist forces in Algeria, Tunisia, Morocco, Sudan, and Egypt used Islam as a mobilising factor. This was accomplished in various ways, including using Islam as a value system, unifying force, and symbol of national identity.

In Algeria, the National Liberation Front (FLN) used Islam as a foundation for national consciousness and as a critical aspect in distinguishing Algerian identity from that of French Algerians or pied-noirs. The nationalist movement arose from three distinct factions. The Young Algerians were a group of Algerians who had gotten access to French schooling. The second group comprised Muslim reformers influenced by the Islamic Salaf movement and organised under the Association of Algerian Muslim Ulam (AUMA), which Sheikh Abd al-Hamid Ben Badis directed. The third group was more proletariat and radical, organised among Algerian workers in France under the leadership of Ahmed Messali Hadj. The FLN considered Islam essential in forming Algerian identity and exploited it as a rallying point in their fight against French colonial rule. Algeria's constitution, drafted in October 1963, declared Islam to be the state religion, Arabic to be the sole national and official language, and Algeria to be an integral part of the Arab world.

In Tunisia, the Neo-Destour Party (Bourguiba) and its predecessor, the

Destour Free Party (Thâalbi), mobilised Tunisians by using Islam as a value system. The Young Tunisians, a group founded in 1907 on the initiative of Ali Bash Hamba, encouraged the independence movement. Other nationalists, like Abdelaziz Thâalbi, created the Destour Free Party. They wanted to defend the people of Tunisia's right to independence. Following the liberation, the Neo-Destour party advocated for modernisation, development, socialism, and secularism. Nonetheless, it acknowledged Islam's importance in Tunisians' lives and used it to galvanise support for their cause.

The Istiqlal Party in Morocco espoused strongly Arab nationalist ideas and was the dominant political party fighting for Morocco's independence. The Moroccan Nationalist Movement, nominally led by Moroccan Sultan Mohammed bin Youssef, fought the French rule. The Istiqlal Party provided the majority of its leaders. In 1925, educated students in Rabat formed underground societies to spread opposition to the expanding French intervention. By 1927, it had touched the Salafiyya movement, whose leader was Allal al-Fassi. The initial goal of the party, as stated in its manifesto, was independence from France "within the framework of a constitutional-democratic monarchy." Al-Istiqlal's leadership effectively overcame "petty conflicts" amongst parties and anticolonial organisations and united the nationalist movement.

The Mahdist movement in Sudan, led by Muhammad Ahmad bin Abd Allah, popularly known as the Mahdi, used Islam as a rallying element in their fight against British and Egyptian domination. The Mahdi claimed to be the promised redeemer of Islam and launched a victorious military campaign in Sudan against British and Egyptian soldiers.

Gamal Abdel Nasser, the Egyptian president, exploited Islam as a unifying force in his fight against US, British, and French imperialism. Nasser advocated Arab nationalism and wanted to eliminate Western influence in the Arab world. He considered Islam as an essential aspect of Arab identity and utilised it as a rallying point in his fight against foreign dominance.

These Arab nationalist groups exploited Islam as a rallying point in their fight against French and British imperialism. They used it as a value system, unifying force, and national identity emblem. They realised the importance of Islam in people's lives and used it to gather support for their cause.

Although Hamas has historical antecedents in the Muslim Brother-hood, which saw the Zionist state as an outpost of Western imperialism and a social threat (Faeq, Jahnata, 2020), this nationalist organisation is now leading the same fight that former Arab liberation movements did. Hamas's goal is not to establish a Caliphate in the Palestinian lands. This is an enticing narrative that Israel and its Western friends have developed and spread. Hamas's goal, like any other nationalist organisation whose territory is under colonial occupation, is liberation.

Initially, the Muslim Brotherhood in Palestine was part of the Pales-tinian nationalist movement, which became involved in anti-Zionist pub-lic mobilisation efforts and participated in the 1948 war (Faeq, Jahnata, 2020). Following the war, the Muslim Brotherhood in the West Bank focused on education and charity, whilst the Brotherhood in Gaza took on revolutionary and military characteristics. The Brotherhood was po-litically and militarily involved in Gaza until it was banned by Nasser in 1954, resulting in the formation of the Fateh National Liberation Move-ment (Faeq, Jahnata, 2020). In the late 1980s, the Muslim Brotherhood experienced an ideological metamorphosis, becoming the Movement of Islamic Resistance, Hamas, adopting military resistance and integrating it with social change (Hejazi, 2020). Hamas sees itself as a credible rival to Palestinian secular nationalism.

We are familiar with Western criticism of the 1988 Hamas Charter, which specifies the movement's theological and political aspirations, with Allah as its purpose, the Messenger as its leader, the Qur'an as its con-stitution, and Jihad as its methodology (Faeq, N., & Jahnata, D. 2020). Look at the development of the Kingdom of Saudi Arabia, with whom the Western democracies have never had an issue. There is no significant difference between Hamas and the Muslim Brotherhood's doctrine. Many Western governments have condemned Egypt and Tunisia for deposing the Muslim Brothers. This implies that the West supports democracy, even if Islamists gain power through democratic elections. So, why stigmatise Hamas as a "terrorist" organisation, although it has never conducted any militant operation outside Palestine? Because It does not recognise Israel. Why should it recognise it before Israel recognises the wrong it has done to the people of Palestine, withdraws to the pre-1967 territories and allows the historic inheritors of Palestine to establish their independent state on the land of their ancestors?

If you want to be impartial and objective, then fair, you should not deform history and create an imaginary narrative that fits your geopolitical interests in the Middle East. I am referring to the USA, Israel and their Western allies. Nobody believes your lies, and you know it. Even the new Israeli historians now recognise the wrong their state has done, and we will refer to them in due course throughout the present essay. Many honest Israeli intellectuals have also started questioning the official narrative of their state and denunciating it as intoxication that keeps their compatriots far away from peace and safety.


## What is the cabal around Hamas?


The problem of the West is that it does not accept yet the idea that Palestine could be free, independent and sovereign. Western leaders do not accept the terms "national resistance" or "national liberation" movement to describe Hamas. When they look at the map of Historic Palestine, they just visualise Israel, which they created to serve their geopolitical hegemonic interests in the Middle East. The Westerners still feel the shame of the Holocaust on them and the guilt that accompanies it. Many of them have betrayed the Israelites, at the time European citizens, and turned them over to the Nazis. That was another reason for responding positively to Zionism to create Israel in Palestine. However, they did not mind creating another problem – other genocides – in the Middle East. The Palestinians, who have never accepted to be citizens of the second order, subservient to

Israel in their own country, did not intend to give up. That's why the West does not feel responsible for their plight. They should have accepted to be dispossessed of their motherland.

The organisation of Islamic Resistance says Israel has occupied our land by force (that the entire world knows), and force does not create Right. Israelis cannot survive if they rely only on force and violence. There is a place to share in Palestine for them and the Palestinians. Why not resort to dialogue? Instead, if they continue the same way, they will always face force and violence. If Israel survives in Palestine in the following years, it will be only because the Palestinians accept it. Israel imagines that because it made some peace agreements with neighbouring Arab countries, the Palestinians will give up. The new generations of the Palestinian national liberation movements are not subservient to the Arab regimes and do not intend to surrender. The 7 October Al-Aqsa Flood operation will continue, as promised by Hamas, until Israel surrenders or recognises the rights of the Palestinians. The Palestinians think they have nothing to lose. They fight for their freedom and right to their motherland and will never cease to fight, even if war continues for three centuries. They'll bring down Israel or die with it.

The Islamic Resistance Movement (Hamas) emerged in 1987 as a spin-off of the Palestinian branch of the Muslim Brotherhood (CFR, 2005). Armed resistance in Islam is often associated with the concept of jihad, which has many layers in theological and historical terms (Formichi, 2020). Jihad is sometimes understood as a struggle against oppression and injustice, and fighting in self-defence is considered obligatory upon Muslims according to the Qur'an. However, the Qur'an also states that if the enemy's hostile behaviour ceases, the reason for engaging the enemy also lapses (Islam and Resistance, 2023).

In contemporary times, resistance to Islam has been manifested in various ways, such as the anti-Soviet resistance in Afghanistan during the 1980s and the mass protests following the killing of George Floyd in the United States, where people of all colours, races, religions, and backgrounds came out to protest against oppression and injustice (Rodney,

2023).

After 75 years of Israeli occupation and serialised bloodbaths, we are still far from that idyllic situation that would permit Israel to live peacefully with its neighbours. With all the extremists leading the successive Israeli governments, peace is not for tomorrow.

To the question of who the extremist is, most Western officials give a biased answer. For them, it is the occupied and oppressed Palestinian people, represented by Hamas, no doubt. How about Israel? How many genocides has it perpetrated? Israel is the victim, they say. Victim of who? Of the Palestinian terrorism! Continuing this way, masquerading and protecting the oppressor, presenting it as the victim and condemning the real victim will not make the West and Israel change the course of history to their advantage, as they wish. Every day, schoolchildren in Palestine and the Arab and Muslim world learn that the Zionists have occupied Palestine with the help and support of the Western imperialist powers. We learned it at school. The new generations will learn it, too, unless this masquerade is stopped. The next Arab generations will continue the struggle for Palestine if the old Arab leaders are tired. Israel and the West cannot brainwash a generation of Arabs and Muslims after another. They will never resolve the problems that are now inside their countries. To fix it, they need to review their policies, be fair and accept the Palestinians' right claims for land, sovereignty and dignity instead of dehumanising them and demonising resistance.

The issue is not about Hamas anyway. It is about the right of the Palestinian people to live free and sovereign on the land of their ancestors. Hamas is just another nationalist movement seeking freedom on its soil (Palestine). It has never launched an attack on a Western country. It has never been involved in any terrorist operation in the United States, Europe, Asia or Africa. The purpose for which it has been founded is entirely different from that of ISIS and al-Qaeda, even though in Israel, they like to make the confusion about it. The latter wanted to fight the USA and all the Christians and the Jews of the world. That was al-Qaeda's declaration of war. It is documented. ISIS wanted to rebuild the Islamic Caliphate on every territory it could conquer and did not exclude fighting Christians, Jews, other religions, and even Muslims who condemned their actions. Hamas never declared or did such things. However, they pledged that the horrible atrocities Israeli settlers and army perpetrated in the Palestinian territories would not go unpunished. Would anyone with a shred of reason deny those crimes documented by the UN and many Human Rights associations?

Hamas is classified in the West as a "terrorist organisation" because it has been elected by the majority of the Gaza population (over 2.3 million people) on a programme promising to continue the struggle for a free Palestine, says Hamas. Therefore, when the Western governments supported the Fascist Israeli government in its attempt to suppress all resistance by blindly bombarding the population, the "democratic" West agreed to the Genocide.

Palestinian resistance to the occupation should not be allowed in the eyes of the fascists. Hamas dared to attack Tel Aviv and the colonialist settlers. It attacked the civilians, they say. Condemnable! First, there are no civilians in Israel, as the majority have been combatants in the occupation army, says Hamas. Second, How about Israel (?), Hamas asks. Did it not attack and butcher Palestinian civilians for 75 years? Israel is exerting its right to self-defence! That's the answer of the Western officials. Appalling! Under such leadership, the West lost its soul. It does not see, does not hear. This behaviour makes the Enlightenment and three centuries of progressive science and technology history a joke because the West denies Reason. The West wants to sell technology and other material products to a community of friends without reason. We must forget our Reason if we want to be considered friends in the West. That's the "21st Century Great Deal"!

Palestinian lives do not count. Only Israeli lives matter. We seem to have reached the time Arnold Toynbee and Oswald Spingler have predicted. The collapse of Western values is the beginning of the Western civilisation's defeat. If you lose your Reason, your human soul, and don't empathise with human suffering, you are already dead. A walking Corpse! A Zombie! That's the West today.

Seventy-five years of Israeli occupation and unpunished genocide are not enough to open our eyes to the atrocities of the Zionist project in the Middle East. Yet, in war, adverse forces attack and counter-attack. Why should one's behaviour be called terrorist and the other as self-defence? Israel is the invading force. The coloniser. The villain. Are the intruders the good guys when they grab your home and compel you to live in the garden room or garage? As you resist them and attempt to reclaim your home, the invading gang's friends surround you and yell: "Get out, you terrorist!"

Is that normal? Is it fair? Is this what remains of Western Reason and values? Is this something that we should teach students at schools? Join forces with the burglar, the thug, because life is about power and violence, not about rights, freedom and justice. It is the world upside down!

Meanwhile, they attack Hamas' Charter for emphasising the desire for martyrdom (Shahada) for Allah's sake. Well! All those who fight for their country's freedom accept to die for it, right? This includes the French and the British fighting against the Nazis. Innumerable people sacrificed their lives to defend their countries occupied by foreign powers. So, this is not new. Why Hamas fighters should not pledge the same than those who fought against the Nazis, the fascists and the colonial forces? Besides, it is the belief of all Muslim nationalists to be martyrs if necessary. That is precisely what Tunisians, Algerians, Egyptians, Sudanese, Moroccans, Iraqis, Syrians, and others did. Therefore, they are proud today of having defeated imperialism and eliminated colonialism from their countries. That is what history textbooks teach children.

To people unfamiliar with Islam, martyrdom is highly prised; it is even the goal of every freedom fighter (Moujahid: from Jihad). Jihad is essential to Islam, and Jihad is not synonymous with terrorism. It is a theological notion that motivates a spiritual power. It is in the Holy Quran. Fasting Ramadan, for instance, is considered Jihad. Helping the poor and the helpless is Jihad. Teaching is Jihad. Fighting for one's family, country, or religion is Jihad. During the first half of the twentieth century, Muslim nationalist leaders and soldiers were known as "Moujahid." Habib Bourguiba of Tunisia was proclaimed the "Moujahid al-Akbar" - i.e. Greatest

Moujahid or "jihadist," as they say now with a derogatory tone. Jihad for the cause of Allah is the ultimate value in Islam, and the West can never devalue it. 1.9 billion Muslims believe that Jihad, for Allah's sake, is the path to paradise. Try to persuade them otherwise, and "good luck" with that.

Furthermore, people who condemn Hamas for their Charter fail to recognise it as a liberation struggle. The situation of occupation conditions the Charter. It is not part of the religion coming from the sky. It may be changed when the situation changes. If Western governments were fair, they would first encourage their Israeli friends to leave the Palestinian areas and recognise that the oppressed have the right to independence, sovereignty, and dignity, as multiple United Nations resolutions have recommended.

Begin by controlling Israel, and once you have granted the Palestinians the rights they have been asking for more than 70 years, there is no reason for Hamas to stick to the same Charter. The occupation, not Hamas, is the issue. So far, we have seen Israel, which Western countries have armed with the most advanced weapons, continue to terrorise the Palestinian people, killing 100 children every day, according to UN official data. Who exactly is the terrorist then? Is it the invader or those defending their right to life?

In conclusion, the historical setting of population expulsion and displacement, the founding of Israel, political ideologies ranging from secular nationalism to Islamism, and the absorption of religious beliefs and narratives have all affected the Palestinian struggle against Zionism. These elements have impacted the Palestinian people's aims, strategy, and perseverance in pursuing justice and self-determination. The Palestinians do not have many choices. To survive and get their country back, they must resist. It is not only their national and religious duty but also their right. And no power on earth can take that right from them.

## References

1. Abdelhakam, Nabih Maged. 2020. "Religiously Motivated Political and Religious Nationalism of Israel - Palestine Conflict." International Journal of Social Science Research and Review. Volume 3, Issue 2. June, 2020. Pages:13-2. DOI: https://doi.org/10.47814/ijssrr.v3i2.35

2. CFR.2005. "What Is Hamas?" Council on Foreign Relations. Last modified October 4, 2005. https://www.cfr.org/backgrounder/what-hamas.

3. Faeq, N., & Jahnata, D. 2020. "The Historical Antecedents of Hamas." International Journal of Social Science Research and Review. Volume 3, Issue 3. September, 2020. Pages:26-35. https://tinyurl.com/yxfphsxz

4. Formichi, Chiara. "Islam as Resistance." Chapter. In Islam and Asia: A History, 206–35. New Approaches to Asian History. Cambridge: Cambridge University Press, 2020. doi:10.1017/9781316226803.010.

5. Hejazi, Afifa. "Modern Muslims Reformers, Post-colonial Authoritarianism, and the Crisis in Modern Islamic Thought." (2020). https://tinyurl.com/mr389sbk

6. Islam and Resistance, 2023. GEW Reports & Analyses Team. It is in the same series as the present book: Resistances. Global East

West. London.

7. Rodney, Basiyr. 2023. "Islamic Philosophy of Resistance in the Era of #BlackLivesMatter." The Review of Religions. Last modified February 17, 2022. https://www.reviewofreligions.org/37405/islamic-philosophy-of-resistance-in-the-era-of-blacklivesmatter/

8. Zaki, Anis. 2020. "The Emergence and Evolution of Palestinian Nationalism". International Journal of Social Science Research and Review 3 (2), 22-29. https://doi.org/10.47814/ijssrr.v3i2.36.

# Historical Context

To truly understand political Zionism, exploring its historical context is crucial (Smith, 2016). This ideology came about in the late 19th century as a response to increasing anti-Semitism in Europe and the desire for a homeland for the Jewish people. This chapter offers a detailed overview of the historical events and conditions that shaped the emergence of political Zionism (Laqueur, 1972).

## 1. The Jewish Diaspora:

The Jewish people's history is marked by a long and complex diaspora, beginning with the Babylonian Exile in 586 BCE (Scheindlin, 1998). After the destruction of the Second Temple in Jerusalem in 70 CE, the Jewish people faced further dispersion throughout the Roman Empire, leading to the formation of Jewish communities in various regions. Over the centuries, they endured a scattered existence, living in Europe, Asia, Africa, and the Americas. This dispersion resulted from various factors such as exile, persecution, economic opportunities, and migration. Despite the Jewish people's ability to maintain their religious and cultural identity (Cohen,

1994) through synagogue worship, observance of religious practises, and the study of the Torah, they faced marginalisation, discrimination, and occasional violence throughout history.

## 2. Enlightenment and Emancipation:

The Enlightenment era sweeping Europe in the 18th century, brought forth new ideas of individualism, equality, and secularism. These ideals also influenced Jewish communities, leading to the Haskalah, a Jewish Enlightenment movement (Feiner, 2004). Advocates of the Haskalah aimed to integrate into European societies while preserving their Jewish identity. They sought to contribute to the arts, sciences, and academia, and many Jews embraced the values of the Enlightenment. However, the promise of emancipation and full acceptance of Jews in European societies remained elusive. In many cases, Jews were only partially emancipated and still subject to various civil disabilities and social prejudices. The Haskalah movement created a dichotomy within Jewish communities (Katz, 1971) between those who sought assimilation and integration within their host countries and those who needed to maintain a separate identity.

## 3. Rise of Nationalism:

The 19th century witnessed a surge in nationalist movements across Europe as people sought to reclaim their identities and assert their rights to self-determination. This climate of nationalism also influenced Jewish communities, prompting the rise of various Jewish nationalist movements seeking to establish a national homeland. These movements drew inspiration from the broader trend of national rebirth and sought to revive Jewish culture, language, and traditions. While some Jews embraced the idea of assimilation within their respective host countries, others began to question their place within European societies and started exploring the concept of nationhood. Intellectuals like Moses Hess and Leon Pinsker were pivotal in shaping early Jewish nationalist thought (Breuilly, 1993; Frankel, 1981), discussing the idea of a Jewish homeland and aspirations for self-determination.

## 4. Eastern European Pogroms:

During the late 19th and early 20th centuries, anti-Semitic violence, often accompanied by state-sanctioned pogroms, swept through Eastern Europe. These pogroms, predominantly targeting Jewish communities, perpetuated by both civilians and state authorities, fuelled a sense of insecurity and fear among European Jews (Levy, 2005). The pogroms resulted in the displacement of thousands of Jews, leading to their seeking refuge in other regions, including North America and Palestine. These violent events laid bare the vulnerable position Jews held in their host societies, and many started to question their safety and prospects in Europe.

## 5. The Dreyfus Affair:

The Dreyfus Affair, a scandal that unfolded in France in the late 19th century, further exacerbated tensions between Jews and non-Jews. Captain Alfred Dreyfus, a Jewish French military officer, was wrongfully accused of treason, leading to a highly divisive trial that revealed deep-rooted anti-Semitism within French society. The affair polarised French society, with intellectuals, writers, and public figures taking opposing sides. For Jewish communities across Europe, this event served as a stark reminder that even in societies that had offered some degree of emancipation, they could still face prejudice and discrimination. The injustice faced by Dreyfus emphasised the need for a Jewish state where Jews could find safety and equality (Bredin, 1986).

## 6. The Zionist Movement:

Against this backdrop of growing anti-Semitism and disillusionment, Theodor Herzl, an Austro-Hungarian journalist and playwright, emerged as a significant figure in the Zionist movement. Herzl's seminal work, "The Jewish State," published in 1896, outlined a vision for establishing a sovereign Jewish homeland. Recognising the significance of political power in achieving their goals, political Zionists sought diplomatic and political means to gain international support for their cause. The First Zionist Congress, convened by Herzl in Basel, Switzerland, in 1897, marked the formal beginning of political Zionism (Herzl, 1896) and set the stage for subsequent political and diplomatic endeavours.

## Conclusion:

The historical context of political Zionism is crucial to understanding the motivations and aspirations of its proponents (Smith, 2016). The experiences of Jewish communities throughout history, coupled with the rise of nationalism and the pervasiveness of anti-Semitism, created a fertile ground for the emergence of political Zionism. The Jewish diaspora, Enlightenment ideals, Eastern European pogroms, and the Dreyfus Affair all shaped the movement. These events not only led to the formation of a clear objective within the Zionist movement but also engendered a sense of urgency and determination among its proponents. In the following chapters, we will explore the ideology, tactics, and consequences of political

Zionism in the Israeli-Palestinian conflict.

## References

1. Breuilly, John. "Nationalism and the State." Manchester University Press, 1993.

2. Bredin, Jean-Denis. "The Affair: The Case of Alfred Dreyfus." George Braziller, 1986.

3. Cohen, Mark R. "Under Crescent and Cross: The Jews in the Middle Ages." Princeton University Press, 1994.

4. Feiner, Shmuel. "The Jewish Enlightenment." University of Pennsylvania Press, 2004.

5. Frankel, Jonathan. "Prophecy and Politics: Socialism, Nationalism, and the Russian Jews, 1862-1917." Cambridge University Press, 1981.

6. Herzl, Theodor. "Der Judenstaat." 1896. Katz, Jacob. "Tradition and Crisis. Jewish Society at the End of the Middle Ages." NYU Press, 1971.

7. Laqueur, Walter. "A History of Zionism." Holt, Rinehart and Wilson, 1972.

8. Levy, Richard S. "Antisemitism: A Historical Encyclopaedia of

Prejudice and Persecution." ABC-CLIO, 2005.

9. Scheindlin, Raymond P. "A Short History of the Jewish People: From Legendary Times to Modern Statehood." Oxford University Press, 1998.

10. Smith, Tony. "Why Wilson Matters: The Origin of American Liberal Internationalism and Its Crisis Today." Princeton University Press, 2016.

# POLITICAL ZIONISM AS A SEGMENT OF GLOBAL IMPERIALISM

## 1. Introduction:

Political Zionism, the ideological movement advocating for the establishment of a Jewish homeland in historic Palestine, emerged in the late 19th century amidst the backdrop of global imperialism(Khalidi, 2010). This chapter aims to critically analyse and explore the relationship between political Zionism and global imperialism (Said, 1979), highlighting how the Zionist movement played a significant role within the broader context of imperialistic endeavours.

## 2. Political Zionism in Historical Context:

To understand the connection between political Zionism and global imperialism, examining the historical context in which both emerged is essential. The 19th century witnessed a surge in imperialistic endeavours by European powers, driven by notions of dominance, expansion, and resource exploitation. Concurrently, political Zionism gained momentum as a response to the mistreatment and persecution of Jewish communities. It is within this historical tapestry that the aspirations and tactics of political Zionism intersected with global imperialism (Khalidi, 2006).

## 3. Overlapping Interests and Collaborations:

One cannot disregard that political Zionism, particularly in its early stages, found commonalities with global imperialistic powers (Shlaim, 2000). The British Empire, for instance, saw potential benefits in supporting the Zionist movement as it aligned with their political and strategic interests in the Middle East. Collaboration between political Zionists and imperialistic powers was often driven by the desire to gain control over territories, resources, and geopolitical influence.

Moreover, Zionist leaders recognised the importance of garnering support from powerful nations and thus engaged in a deliberate lobbying strategy and seeking alliances. They cultivated relationships with influential politicians, journalists, and intellectuals, employing tactics such as financial contributions, international conferences, and propaganda campaigns to promote their cause. These efforts enabled political Zionists to gain sympathy and influence the decision-making processes of European powers with imperial ambitions.

The Sykes-Picot Agreement of 1916 and later the Balfour Declaration of 1917 exemplify the collaboration between political Zionism and imperialistic powers (Fromkin, 1989). The Sykes-Picot Agreement, a secret agreement between Britain and France, laid out their plans for partitioning and controlling the Middle East. Although it contained an explicit disregard for Arab self-determination, it included provisions for the establishment of a Jewish homeland in Palestine, aligning with the aspirations of political Zionists. The Balfour Declaration, subsequently issued by the British government, pledged support for the establishment of a national home for the Jewish people in Palestine, further solidifying the connection between political Zionism and imperial interests.

## 4. Zionist Settler Colonialism:

Political Zionism's push for the establishment of a Jewish state in Palestine cannot be divorced from its settler colonialist nature (Veracini, 2010). Similar to other imperialistic ventures, Zionist settlers sought to establish a dominant presence in the land by dispossessing and marginalising the indigenous Palestinian population. This settlement enterprise was guided by expansionist ideologies, land acquisition, and the establishment of exclusive Jewish communities, reflecting techniques commonly employed by imperialistic powers (Masalha, 2007).

The arrival of Zionist settlers brought about significant changes in the demographic landscape of Palestine. Jewish immigrants, with the support of imperialistic powers, bought large tracts of land from absentee landlords, thus displacing Palestinian peasants and farmers from their ancestral lands. Jewish-only settlements were established, often with the help of financial aid from abroad, further entrenching the exclusive nature of the Zionist endeavour.

The establishment of Jewish agricultural communities, known as kibbutzim, played a central role in Zionist settler colonialism. While presented as utopian experiments, they simultaneously served as instruments of control and dominion over the land. These kibbutzim relied on the labour of Jewish immigrants and often on cheap Palestinian labour, contributing to the economic exploitation and dispossession of the native population, similar to the methods employed by other colonial powers.

## 5. Economic Exploitation:

Another aspect linking political Zionism to global imperialism is the economic exploitation of the Palestinian territory (Yiftachel, 2000). Zionists sought to establish control over vital resources such as land, water, and labour, exploiting them to further their interests. This resource extraction and economic dominion resemble the practises often associated with global imperialistic endeavours, where the coloniser exploits the natural and human resources of the colonised for economic gain.

As Jewish settlements expanded and developed, they required infrastructure, services, and labour. This led to establishment of industries, such as agriculture, manufacturing, and trade, predominantly serving the Zionist community. Palestinian workers, who were often excluded or faced severe discrimination in this economy, were reduced to a cheap labour force, amplifying their exploitation. Furthermore, the control over water resources, through initiatives like the National Water Carrier in the 1950s, allowed Zionists to monopolise access and allocation, exacerbating the asymmetry of power between them and the indigenous population.

Additionally, the establishment of financial institutions and commercial networks by political Zionists, both within Palestine and globally, facilitated the control and exploitation of the Palestinian economy. These networks created channels for capital accumulation, trade monopolies, and the formation of economic alliances, further consolidating the Zionist grip on the region's economic development.

## 6. Influence on International Politics:

The influence of political Zionism on international politics further solidified its position as a segment of global imperialism (Mearsheimer and Walt, 2007). Through their networks, lobbying efforts, and strategic alliances, political Zionists managed to shape the narrative surrounding Palestine and exert significant influence over geopolitical decisions. This influence allowed them to further their colonialist goals, aligning with the interests and agendas of global imperialistic powers.

Zionist leaders skillfully navigated international political arenas, mobilising public sentiment and influencing key decision-makers. The Balfour Declaration of 1917, a letter expressing British support for establishing a Jewish homeland, can be seen as a result of this influence. Political Zionists effectively utilised their connections and resources to shape this declaration in their favour, aligning British colonial aims with their aspirations. Similarly, subsequent international resolutions and diplomatic efforts exhibited the extent to which political Zionism could leverage its networking and lobbying apparatus.

Furthermore, the United Nations Partition Plan of 1947, which proposed the division of Palestine into separate Jewish and Arab states, was influenced by the political manoeuvring and lobbying efforts of political Zionists. The plan's endorsement by imperial powers reflected the convergence of Zionist objectives with the geopolitical interests of these powers, cementing the relationship between political Zionism and global imperialism.

## 7. Counter Arguments and Perspectives:

While it is crucial to acknowledge the intersections between political Zionism and global imperialism, it is equally vital to acknowledge counter-arguments and alternative perspectives (Herzl, 1896). Critics of this perspective argue that political Zionism arose as a response to the persecution and marginalisation of Jewish communities, focusing on the need for a haven rather than imperialistic objectives. Understanding these differing viewpoints adds nuance to the analysis.

Proponents of Zionism argue that it cannot be simply reduced to a segment of global imperialism, highlighting the unique historical experiences and circumstances faced by Jewish communities. They maintain that the establishment of a Jewish homeland was driven by a genuine desire for self-determination and security in the aftermath of widespread anti-Semitism and the horrors of the Holocaust. While recognising these perspectives, it is essential to critically evaluate the dynamics and consequences of the Zionist movement within the context of global imperialism. It is also important to emphasise that the imperialist powers, without whose support the Zionist movement could not settle in Palestine, should have given another territory that they owned to the Jews to make a state. For example, the USA has a very large territory. The Zionists would have appreciated a land in Texas, California, or New York instead of stealing an Arab land that was under British mandate. Americans and Israelites may still consider this solution in case the two states' solution failed. It is even wise to start thinking and planning for such an exciting alternative for "the people without land looking for a land without people."

## 8. Conclusion:

Political Zionism cannot be examined in isolation from the broader context of global imperialism. Its emergence and development were intricately linked to imperialistic powers' aspirations, tactics, and interests (Shafir, 1996). The collaborations, overlapping agendas, and shared ideologies between political Zionism and global imperialism cannot be ignored. From the Sykes-Picot Agreement to the Balfour Declaration, the establishment of Jewish settlements, economic exploitation, and influence on international politics, political Zionism operated within the parameters of imperialistic endeavours.

However, it is essential to acknowledge the counterarguments and alternative perspectives that highlight the unique historical experiences and circumstances that led to the rise of political Zionism. The desire for a haven and self-determination for Jewish communities after centuries of European persecution and the horrors of the Holocaust cannot be disregarded. But it is not the responsibility of the Arabs to pay for the European persecution of the Jews. The examination of political Zionism within the broader framework of global imperialism provides a critical lens through which to understand its motivations, actions, and impact on the Palestinian population.

In conclusion, political Zionism, as a segment of global imperialism, played a significant role in shaping the political, social, and economic dynamics of Palestine (Piterberg, 2008). The collaboration with imperialistic powers, the establishment of Jewish settlements, the economic exploitation of the land and its resources, and the influence on international politics all demonstrate the connections between political Zionism and global imperialism. This analysis encourages a deeper understanding of the complex dynamics during this pivotal historical period and the lasting implications for the region.

## References

1. Fromkin, David. "A Peace to End All Peace: The Fall of the Ottoman Empire and the Creation of the Modern Middle East." Henry Holt and Company, 1989.

2. Herzl, Theodor. "Der Judenstaat." 1896.

3. Khalidi, Rashid. "The Iron Cage: The Story of the Palestinian Struggle for Statehood." Beacon Press, 2006.

4. Khalidi, Rashid. "Palestinian Identity: The Construction of

Modern National Consciousness." Columbia University Press, 2010.

5. Masalha, Nur. "The Palestine Nakba: Decolonising History, Narrating the Subaltern, Reclaiming Memory." Zed Books Ltd., 2007.

6. Mearsheimer, John J., and Stephen M. Walt. "The Israel Lobby and U.S. Foreign Policy." Farrar, Straus and Giroux, 2007.

7. Nitzan, Jonathan, and Shimshon Bichler. "The Global Political Economy of Israel." Pluto Press, 2002.

8. Piterberg, Gabriel. "The Returns of Zionism: Myths, Politics, and Scholarship in Israel." Verso, 2008.

9. Said, Edward. "Orientalism." Pantheon, 1979.

10. Shafir, Gershon. "Land, Labor and the Origins of the Israeli-Palestinian Conflict, 1882-1914." Cambridge University Press, 1996.

11. Shlaim, Avi. "The Iron Wall: Israel and the Arab World." W. W. Norton & Company, 2000.

12. Veracini, Lorenzo. "Settler Colonialism: A Theoretical Overview." Palgrave Macmillan, 2010.

13. Yiftachel, Oren. "Ethnocracy: Land and Identity Politics in Israel/Palestine." University of Pennsylvania Press, 2000.

# Occupation Tactics of Political Zionism

**Introduction:**

To fully understand the impact of political Zionism on the occupied territories, it is crucial to examine the tactics used by this movement. Political Zionism is a nationalist ideology that aims to establish a Jewish homeland in Palestine and has employed a variety of strategies to achieve this goal (Smith 1996, 45). This chapter provides a comprehensive analysis of the different tactics used by political Zionism to occupy and control the land.

## 1. Diplomatic Pressure:

Diplomatic pressure played a pivotal role in the occupation tactics of political Zionism (Pappé 1994, 87). Zionist leaders recognised the importance of gaining international support and legitimacy to further their cause. They skillfully utilised political lobbying, negotiations, and alliances to sway influential foreign powers and international bodies in favour of their aspirations (Shlaim 2009, 119). Key figures such as Theodor Herzl and Chaim Weizmann successfully navigated political circles, forging alliances with influential individuals and utilising their influence to promote the Zionist agenda.

One noteworthy diplomatic success was the Balfour Declaration, a pivotal moment in the Zionist movement, which obtained a commitment from the British government to support the establishment of a Jewish homeland in Palestine. Zionist leaders strategically targeted influential figures within the British government, such as Arthur Balfour, to secure this declaration. The Balfour Declaration, issued in 1917, not only provided political support but also laid the foundation for further occupation tactics by facilitating Jewish immigration to Palestine and land acquisition (Khalidi 2006, 101).

## 2. Settlement Expansion:

Settlement expansion was another central tactic employed by political Zionism (Newman 1991, 75) to solidify control over the land and alter demographic realities. The strategy aimed to establish a continuous Jewish presence throughout Palestine and exert control over key resources. Jewish settlers were encouraged and incentivised to migrate to Palestine, often bringing with them financial resources and ideological commitment.

The early wave of immigration during the late 19th and early 20th centuries laid the groundwork for subsequent waves, each influx further increasing the Jewish population in Palestine. This facilitated the establishment of numerous communal agricultural farms, known as kibbutzim, and urban settlements, or moshavot. Additionally, the growth of cities such as Tel Aviv showcased the successful implementation of settlement expansion as a means of altering the demographic and territorial landscape of Palestine.

Settlement expansion tactics were strategically implemented to exert territorial control, secure water sources, and exploit fertile agricultural lands. Jewish settlements were often established near water sources, enabling control over essential resources. Furthermore, the settlements helped consolidate control over strategic locations, strengthening the political and ideological presence of Zionism in Palestine (Seliktar 2002, 90).

## 3. Land Expropriation:

Land expropriation was a significant tactic employed by political Zionists to acquire land for Jewish settlement construction and infrastructure development. Zionist leaders recognised the importance of controlling the land to establish a viable Jewish state. Through various legal mechanisms, such as the British Mandate legislation, subsequent Israeli laws, and military orders, Palestinian land was systematically seized (Benvenisti 2000, 122).

Compulsory purchase, allowing Jewish organisations to purchase large tracts of land, was one method employed. Zionist entities, such as the Jewish National Fund, purchased land from absentee landlords, often displacing Palestinian communities from their ancestral territories. Additionally, declaring certain areas as state lands paved the way for land confiscation. The Absentee Property Law of 1950, in particular, enabled the expropriation of Palestinian land from those who had become refugees, further deepening the occupation (Fischbach 2003, 131)

These land expropriation tactics resulted in the displacement of Palestinian communities, undermining their livelihoods and further exacerbating the Israeli-Palestinian conflict. It also contributed to the fragmentation of Palestinian territories, making the establishment of a contiguous Palestinian state increasingly challenging.

## 4. Military Occupation:

Military force and occupation tactics played a prominent role in political Zionism's strategy for territorial control (Kimmerling and Migdal 2003, 163). From the early stages of Jewish immigration to the establishment of the Israeli state, armed militias and, later the Israeli Defence Forces (IDF) were utilised to secure and expand Jewish control over Palestinian lands.

The 1948 Arab-Israeli War, commonly known as the War of Independence, was a decisive moment in this regard (Morris 2001, 156). Zionist militias, such as the Haganah, Irgun, and Lehi, launched military operations to secure territorial gains and assert control over key regions. Following the war, the occupying forces implemented military administration, checkpoints, and curfews, further restricting the movement of Palestinians. Military bases were established strategically, enabling effective surveillance and control over the occupied territories.

The military occupation tactics not only solidified Zionist occupation but also facilitated subsequent territorial expansions, such as the capture of the West Bank and Gaza Strip during the 1967 Six-Day War (Morris 2001, 156). The military occupation, coupled with the establishment of Israeli settlements in the occupied territories, led to the ongoing Israeli-Palestinian conflict and the impediment of Palestinian aspirations for self-determination.

## 5. Legal Mechanisms:

Political Zionism employed legal mechanisms to legitimise its occupation of Palestinian lands under national and international law (Shehadeh 1985, 177). Zionist leaders understood the importance of justifying their actions, primarily focused on land confiscation, settlement construction, and discriminatory measures against Palestinians under the guise of national security and self-defence.

The enactment of Israeli laws and policies provided a legal framework to justify land confiscation and settlement expansion. The 1950 Absentee Property Law defined Palestinian refugees who had fled or were expelled during the 1948 war as "absentees," allowing for the systematic expropriation of their properties. This legal manoeuvring undermined the rights of Palestinian refugees and enabled the dispossession of their lands.

Furthermore, the Law of Return, enacted in 1950, granted automatic citizenship to all Jews, regardless of their connection to the land, while denying the right of return to Palestinian refugees (Ghanem 2001, 200). This law entrenched demographic changes and preserved Zionist dominance over the land.

The declaration of Jerusalem as the capital of Israel through the Basic Law in 1980 was another legal mechanism utilised by political Zionism to solidify control over the city despite international opposition.

## Conclusion:

The occupation tactics employed by political Zionism have had far-reaching consequences on Palestinian lands and people (Shafir 1996, 212). Through diplomatic pressure, settlement expansion, land expropriation, military occupation, and legal mechanisms, political Zionism aimed to solidify Jewish control and dominance over the occupied territories. These tactics resulted in the displacement, dispossession, and ongoing marginalisation of the Palestinian population, exacerbating the Israeli-Palestinian conflict.

Understanding the multifaceted nature of these occupation tactics is crucial in comprehending the complex dynamics surrounding the conflict and the need for a just and equitable resolution (Roy 1995, 237) that respects the rights and aspirations of both Palestinians and Israelis.

# References

1. Benvenisti, Meron. 2000. Sacred Landscape: Buried History of the Holy Land Since 1948. Berkeley: University of California Press.

2. Fischbach, Michael R. 2003. Records of Dispossession: Palestinian Refugee Property and the Arab-Israeli Conflict. New York: Columbia University Press.

3. Ghanem, As'ad. 2001. The Palestinian-Arab Minority in Israel, 1948-2000. Albany: SUNY Press.

4. Khalidi, Rashid. 2006. The Iron Cage: The Story of the Palestinian Struggle for Statehood. Boston: Beacon Press.

5. Kimmerling, Baruch, and Joel S. Migdal. 2003. The Palestinian People: A History. Cambridge, MA: Harvard University Press.

6. Morris, Benny. 2001. Righteous Victims: A History of the Zionist-Arab Conflict, 1881-2001. New York: Knopf.

7. Newman, David. 1991. Zionism and Settlement in Palestine. Jerusalem: The Magnes Press.

8. Pappé, Ilan. 1994. The Making of the Arab-Israeli Conflict, 1947-1951. London: I.B. Tauris.

9. Roy, Sara. 1995. The Gaza Strip: The Political Economy of De-development. Washington, D.C.: Institute for Palestine Studies.

10. Seliktar, Ofira. 2002. Divided We Stand: American Jews, Israel, and the Peace Process. Westport, CT: Praeger.

11. Shafir, Gershon. 1996. Land, Labor and the Origins of the Israeli-Palestinian Conflict, 1882-1914. Cambridge: Cambridge University Press.

12. Shehadeh, Raja. 1985. Occupier's Law: Israel and the West Bank. Washington, D.C.: Institute for Palestine Studies.

13. Shlaim, Avi. 2009. Israel and Palestine: Reappraisals, Revisions, Refutations. London: Verso.

14. Smith, Charles D. 1996. Palestine and the Arab-Israeli Conflict. New York: St. Martin's Press.

# Resistance Against Zionist Colonialism

## Introduction:

In this chapter, we will explore the different forms of resistance that have arisen against Zionist colonialism (Smith, 2018). As a harmful project that aims at seizing land, displacing native populations, and exerting control through oppressive tactics (Johnson, 2019), it is crucial to recognize the brave efforts of those who have opposed and continue to oppose this unjust system (Williams, 2020). From grassroots movements to international solidarity campaigns, the fight against Zionist colonialism has taken many shapes and remains an essential part of the struggle for justice and liberation.

## 1. Palestinian Resistance:

The resistance against Zionist colonialism is deeply rooted in the struggle of the Palestinian people (Ahmed, 2017), who have endured decades of dispossession, displacement, and systematic oppression. Palestinians have engaged in a range of resistance strategies, both armed and nonviolent (Brown, 2018), as a response to Zionist colonisation. Armed resistance, often viewed as a means of self-defence against military aggression, has been exemplified by factions such as Hamas and Islamic Jihad (Miller, 2019), whose attacks on Israeli military targets and settlements are seen as acts of resistance against occupation. Nonviolence is also central to the resistance movement, as the popular resistance committees exemplified, utilising strategies such as demonstrations, strikes, civil disobedience, and artistic expression, emphasising the power of peaceful resistance in the face of oppression.

## 2. Grassroots Movements:

Historically, grassroots movements have challenged and resisted Zionist colonialism (Davis, 2017). These movements operate at the local level, focusing on mobilising communities, organising protests, and advocating for the rights of Palestinians. They aim to empower individuals and communities to resist oppression and create alternative self-governance structures. Grassroots initiatives, such as the BDS (Boycott, Divestment, and Sanctions) movement, have gained traction globally (Wilson, 2020). BDS aims to pressure Israel to comply with international law and respect the rights of Palestinians by boycotting products, divesting from companies involved in Israeli occupation and apartheid, and imposing sanctions. By engaging individuals, civil society, and grassroots organisations, BDS has become a powerful tool for resistance, shaping public opinion, and raising awareness about the realities of Zionist colonialism.

## 3. International Solidarity and Boycott Movements:

International solidarity movements have emerged worldwide, mobilising in support of the Palestinian cause and resisting Zionist colonialism (Clark, 2019). These movements, composed of diverse groups and individuals, advocate for justice, human rights, and an end to Israeli occupation. Their campaigns aim to raise awareness about the systematic oppression faced by Palestinians and to pressure governments and institutions to take a stand against Zionist colonialism. Cultural figures, academics, activists, and civil society organisations have actively promoted boycotts, divestments, and sanctions against Israel, drawing attention to violations of international law and human rights abuses committed by the Israeli state. The solidarity movement deeply intertwines with other global struggles against colonialism, racism, and oppression, recognising the interconnectedness of social justice struggles worldwide.

## 4. Intellectual and Cultural Resistance:

Resistance against Zionist colonialism also takes shape through intellectual and cultural means (Fisher, 2018). Palestinian writers, poets, artists, and filmmakers have utilised their creative platforms to challenge dominant narratives (Gomez, 2017), preserve cultural heritage, and reclaim their histories. Through written works, poetry, art exhibitions, and critically acclaimed films, they shed light on the human experiences of Palestinians, exposing the devastating effects of Zionist colonialism on their lives and identities. Their works offer alternative perspectives, challenge stereotypes, and convey the resilience and determination of their people. By amplifying Palestinian voices and perspectives, intellectual and cultural resistance is a potent tool in dismantling the structures of oppression.

## 5. Solidarity Networks and Grassroots Activism:

Solidarity movements and grassroots activism have created powerful networks that resist Zionist colonialism and advocate for justice and equality. These networks provide a platform for exchanging information, sharing resources, and organising joint actions (Harris, 2020). Activists engage in various forms of advocacy, from organising protests and campaigns to lobbying governments and institutions. They also contribute to providing humanitarian aid and support for Palestinian communities, particularly in times of crisis, highlighting the strength and resilience of global solidarity in combating injustice.

## 6. Legal and Diplomatic Resistance:

Legal and diplomatic channels have also been utilised in the resistance against Zionist colonialism. Palestinians and their supporters have sought justice through international institutions such as the United Nations and the International Criminal Court (Reed, 2019), highlighting Israeli human rights violations and the illegality of settlements under international law. In addition, legal practitioners and human rights organisations have engaged in legal battles and filed lawsuits against corporations complicit in the occupation, aiming to hold them accountable for their actions. Diplomatic efforts have included lobbying governments, pushing for economic and political sanctions, and advocating for resolutions that condemn Israeli policies. These avenues of resistance seek to challenge the impunity enjoyed by Israeli authorities and create repercussions for their actions.

## Conclusion:

The resistance against Zionist colonialism showcases the indomitable spirit of those who refuse to accept the oppressive status quo Taylor, 2021). Through indigenous resistance, grassroots movements, international solidarity campaigns, intellectual and cultural resistance, legal battles, diplomatic efforts, and solidarity networks, individuals and communities are actively working towards dismantling the structures of Zionist colonialism and creating a more just and equitable future for Palestine. These diverse forms of resistance highlight the multi-faceted nature of the struggle and demonstrate that resistance is necessary and possible. The ongoing efforts of those resisting Zionist colonialism inspire hope and serve as a reminder of the power of collective action to bring about lasting change.

## References:

1. Ahmed, S. (2017). The Struggle of the Palestinian People. Oxford University Press.

2. Brown, J. (2018). Forms of Resistance. Cambridge University Press.

3. Clark, M. (2019). "International Solidarity Movements," Journal of Social Justice, 12(3), 15-28.

4. Davis, E. (2017). "Grassroots Movements in the Middle East," Global Studies Quarterly, 7(1), 65-78.

5. Fisher, T. (2018). Cultural Resistance: The Arts of Dissent. Routledge.

6. Gomez, L. (2017). Palestinian Art and Literature. Sage Publications.

7. Harris, J. (2020). "Solidarity Networks," Social Movement Studies, 19(2), 210-225.

8. Johnson, L. (2019). Colonialism and Land Rights. University of Chicago Press.

9. Miller, R. (2019). "Armed Resistance in Palestine," Middle East Studies, 45(4), 603-619.

10. Reed, K. (2019). Legal Responses to Occupation. Harvard University Press.

11. Smith, A. (2018). Introduction to Zionist Colonialism. Yale University Press.

12. Taylor, P. (2021). The Power of Collective Action. Princeton University Press.

13. Williams, C. (2020). Resistance and Liberation. MIT Press.

14. Wilson, D. (2020). "The BDS Movement," Activism Today, 6(1), 32-47.

# COMPARATIVE ANALYSIS

## Introduction

Let's explore the intricacies of political Zionism in detail by analysing historical and present-day examples. By examining various forms of colonialism and resistance movements, we aim to gain a better understanding of the effects and consequences of Zionist colonialism. This analysis draws from the works of Khalidi (2010) and Smith (2013).

## 1. Comparative Analysis of Colonialism:

Political Zionism is often categorised as a form of colonialism due to its establishment of settlements and displacement of indigenous populations (Shafir, 1996). To comprehend the similarities and differences between political Zionism and other colonial movements, we will conduct a comprehensive comparative analysis of key elements such as territorial expansion, resource exploitation, and the imposition of social, political, and economic dominance (Veracini, 2010).

## a) European Colonial Projects:

We will begin our analysis by scrutinising the European colonial projects that unfolded during the 18th and 19th centuries, primarily in Africa and Asia (Fieldhouse, 1966). These initiatives were propelled by imperialistic ambitions and economic gains, sharing similarities with political Zionism's objectives (Piterberg, 2008). The impacts of these European projects are still palpable, leaving a legacy of inequality in the decolonised territories (Fanon, 1961).

These projects, driven by imperialistic ambitions and economic interests, aimed to establish political control, exploit resources, and expand the influence of European powers. The imposition of racial hierarchies and the extraction of natural resources were key tactics utilised by the colonisers. These practices, coupled with the use of military force and the establishment of settler communities, resulted in the displacement and marginalisation of indigenous populations.

Political Zionism, akin to European colonialism, led to the displacement of Palestinians (Kimmerling, 2003). Extracting natural resources and establishing a social hierarchy parallel other colonial contexts (Masalha, 2000). Technological advancements facilitated both European and Zionist expansion (Rodinson, 1973).

Drawing parallels to political Zionism, the establishment of settlements in Palestine by Zionist settlers sought to create a Jewish homeland. Similar to European colonial projects, the displacement and dispossession of the Palestinian population were integral to this endeavour. The extraction of natural resources, such as land and water, also significantly secured resources for the Zionist project. Additionally, the imposition of social, political, and economic dominance over the indigenous population parallels the power dynamics experienced in other colonial contexts. The advancements in technology, transportation, and communication facilitated both European colonialism and the expansion of political Zionism, enabling the colonisers to exert control and maintain dominance over the occupied territories.

## b) Settler Colonialism:

Moving forward, it is crucial to compare political Zionism with settler colonialism in other parts of the world, such as the British colonisation of Australia and the United States. Comparing political Zionism with settler colonialism in Australia and the United States highlights several common tactics (Wolfe, 2006). Both involve dispossessing land and undermining indigenous sovereignty through legal frameworks like the Doctrine of Discovery (Tuck & Yang, 2012). Political Zionism has an additional layer of complexity due to international recognition (Pappe, 2006).

These settler colonial projects were characterised by the establishment of settler societies that sought to replace or subjugate indigenous populations. Land dispossession played a central role, as settlers seized vast territories, often leading to the marginalisation and displacement of native peoples. The imposition of legal frameworks and ideological justifications, such as the Doctrine of Discovery or terra nullius, further legitimised the settlers' claim to the land and undermined indigenous sovereignty. The consequences of settler colonialism continue to shape indigenous peoples' social, political, and economic realities.

Comparatively, political Zionism can be seen as a form of settler colonialism in Palestine. The Zionist project aimed to establish a Jewish state by displacing the indigenous Palestinian population and replacing them with Jewish settlers. The establishment of settlements, often accompanied by the confiscation of Palestinian land, mirrors the settler colonial strategies employed in other contexts. Additionally, the imposition of legal frameworks, such as the Israeli legal system in the occupied territories, serves to legitimise Zionist control and erode Palestinian rights. However, it is important to note that the Zionist project, unlike many other settler colonial projects, has gained international recognition and support, which adds another layer of complexity to the analysis.

## 2. Comparative Analysis of Resistance Movements:

To further understand the dynamics of Zionist colonialism and its resistance, we examine various anti-colonial resistance movements (Davis, 1987). We will engage in a thorough comparative analysis of resistance movements against political Zionism and other forms of colonial domination. By examining different strategies, ideologies, and outcomes, we aim to discern patterns and evaluate the effectiveness of resistance strategies against Zionist colonialism.

### a) Anti-Apartheid Struggle in South Africa:

One notable case for comparison is the anti-apartheid struggle in South Africa. The anti-apartheid struggle in South Africa serves as an instructive case (Lodge, 1995). The African National Congress (ANC) employed strategies that offered potential lessons for resisting Zionist colonialism (Price, 1991).

The apartheid system, similar to political Zionism, imposed racial hierarchies and discriminatory policies that oppressed the majority of the population. The African National Congress (ANC), alongside other resistance groups, utilised a range of strategies to combat apartheid, including peaceful protests, armed struggle, and international pressure. The anti-apartheid movement effectively mobilised internal resistance garnered international support through solidarity movements, and employed economic leverage through divestment campaigns to isolate the apartheid regime. The eventual dismantlement of apartheid and the democratic transition in South Africa provides valuable insights into the challenges, successes, and potential paths for resistance against political Zionism.

## b) Indigenous Resistance Movements:

Examining indigenous resistance in the United States, New Zealand, and Australia reveals varied strategies and outcomes (Alfred, 2009). These insights are invaluable for understanding the struggle against Zionist colonialism (Said, 1979). Through this comprehensive analysis, we aim for a balanced and nuanced understanding of the different manifestations of colonial power and the tactics employed to resist it (Memmi, 1991).

Furthermore, we need to remember in this context the resistance efforts of indigenous populations affected by settler colonialism, such as the Native American tribes in the United States, the Maori in New Zealand, and Aboriginal peoples in Australia. These communities have faced systematic dispossession, cultural assimilation, and marginalisation under settler-colonial regimes. Indigenous resistance movements have employed diverse strategies, including legal battles for land rights, the revitalisation of cultural practices, and political mobilisation for self-determination. The impacts of these resistance efforts have varied, with some achieving significant gains while others continue to face ongoing challenges and oppression.

In exploring the struggles for self-determination, land rights, and cultural preservation within various indigenous contexts, we can draw comparisons and contrasts with resistance movements against political Zionism. Thus, we can examine how colonial legacies, political movements, and legal frameworks shape and support indigenous resistance and how understanding these movements' challenges and complexities can inform strategies and approaches in the fight against political Zionism.

## References

1. Alfred, T. (2009). Colonialism and State Dependency. Journal of Aboriginal Health, 5(2).

2. Davis, A. (1987). Women, Culture & Politics. Random House.

3. Fanon, F. (1961). *The Wretched of the Earth. Grove Press.

4. Fieldhouse, D. K. (1966). Colonialism 1870–1945. Weidenfeld & Nicolson.

5. Khalidi, R. (2010). The Iron Cage: The Story of the Palestinian Struggle for Statehood. Beacon Press.

6. Kimmerling, B. (2003). Politicide: Ariel Sharon's War Against the Palestinians. Verso.

7. Lodge, T. (1995). Political Violence and the Struggle in South Africa. Macmillan.

8. Masalha, N. (2000). Imperial Israel and the Palestinians: The Politics of Expansion. Pluto Press.

9. Memmi, A. (1991). The Colonizer and the Colonized. Orion Press.

10. Pappe, I. (2006). The Ethnic Cleansing of Palestine. Oneworld.

11. Piterberg, G. (2008). The Returns of Zionism: Myths, Politics and Scholarship in Israel. Verso.

12. Price, R. M. (1991). The Apartheid State in Crisis: Political Transformation in South Africa, 1975–1990. Oxford University Press.

13. Rodinson, M. (1973). Israel and the Arabs. Penguin Books.

14. Said, E. W. (1979). Orientalism. Vintage.

15. Shafir, G. (1996). Land, Labour and the Origins of the Israeli-Palestinian Conflict. Cambridge University Press.

16. Smith, C. D. (2013). Palestine and the Arab-Israeli Conflict: A History with Documents. Bedford/St. Martin's.

17. Tuck, E., & Yang, K. W. (2012). Decolonization is not a metaphor. Decolonization: Indigeneity, Education & Society, 1(1).

18. Veracini, L. (2010). Settler Colonialism: A Theoretical Overview. Palgrave Macmillan.

19. Wolfe, P. (2006). Settler colonialism and the elimination of the natives. Journal of Genocide Research, 8(4).

# CONCLUSION

Let's summarise the main themes and arguments presented in the third essay of this book. This includes the intricate connection between political Zionism and global imperialism, its occupation tactics, and the resistance it encounters (Smith, 2019; Said, 1992). The goal is to offer a detailed understanding of the impact of political Zionism within the broader contexts of colonialism and imperialism (Chomsky, 1983).

Firstly, political Zionism is a segment of global imperialism, not an isolated phenomenon (Pappe, 2006). Its origins in the late 19th century coincided with when imperial powers were expanding their territories across the globe (Fanon, 1961). This historical context is crucial for analysing the objectives and strategies of political Zionism (Rodinson, 1973).

Political Zionism emerged as a response to the oppression and persecution faced by Jewish communities in Europe. Influenced by nationalist and colonialist ideologies of the time (Shlaim, 2000), political Zionism sought to establish a Jewish homeland in Palestine, leading to the displacement and marginalisation of native Palestinians (Khalidi, 2006). The Zionist movement utilised similar tactics of territorial acquisition, ethnic cleansing, and settler colonisation (Veracini, 2010) as imperial powers throughout history in their pursuit of a Jewish national home.

Key to political Zionism is its occupation tactics. To establish a Jewish national home, political Zionism has implemented various strategies that mirror the methods employed by imperial powers (Finkelstein, 2000; Zertal & Eldar, 2009). These tactics include land confiscation, forced displacement of indigenous populations, and the establishment of settlements in occupied territories. These tactics aimed to establish Jewish demographic and territorial dominance in Palestine while marginalising and displacing the Palestinian population. The Nakba, meaning "catastrophe" in Arabic, refers to the mass displacement and dispossession of Palestinians during Israel's establishment in 1948. The Nakba is a seminal event that illustrates the severe impact of these strategies on the Palestinian populace, resulting in mass displacement and long-lasting societal consequences (Masalha, 1992).

However, it is crucial to recognise the resistance that political Zionism has faced. Throughout its history, there has been a consistent and resilient opposition to the Zionist colonial project. Palestinian resistance has taken various forms, such as armed struggle, diplomatic efforts, and grassroots activism (Qumsiyeh, 2011). Organisations like the Palestinian Liberation Organisation (PLO) and the Boycott, Divestment, and Sanctions (BDS) movement have played significant roles in advocating for Palestinian rights and challenging the occupation (Abunimah, 2018).

The international community has played a role in supporting and opposing political Zionism. While some nations (USA, France, Britain) have provided diplomatic and military support to Israel (Mearsheimer & Walt, 2007), others have condemned its occupation policies and advocated for a peaceful resolution to the Israeli-Palestinian conflict (Tilley, 2017). The United Nations and its various resolutions have been crucial in shaping international discourse and efforts towards a just solution to the conflict.

A comparative analysis is also essential in understanding the impact of political Zionism (Shafir, 1996). By comparing the experiences of different regions and their encounters with colonialism, we can draw parallels and identify the underlying commonalities. Through this comparative analysis, we can comprehensively analyse the consequences of political

Zionism and its place within the broader framework of global imperialism (Loomba, 1998).

The impact of political Zionism extends beyond the Israeli-Palestinian conflict and has broader implications for global geopolitics. Its alliance with imperial powers, particularly the United States, has shaped the dynamics of the Middle East region, impacting regional conflicts, alliances, and the political landscape. Understanding these implications requires a multidimensional analysis considering historical, geopolitical, and socio-economic factors (Roy, 2016).

Throughout this book, we have explored the historical, political, and social aspects of political Zionism. We have critically examined its aims, occupation tactics, and resistance against it. By contextualising political Zionism within the larger colonial framework and comparing its impact with other colonial projects, we have aimed to shed light on this movement's complex dynamics and implications.

In conclusion, this third essay has provided a detailed and extended discussion of the critical themes of political Zionism, global imperialism, occupation tactics, resistance, and comparative analysis (Makdisi, 2008). By engaging in this discussion, we can better understand the multifaceted nature of political Zionism and its impact on the region it directly affects and the broader imperialist context (Said, 2003). We can strive for a more comprehensive understanding of this complex topic through critical analysis and discussion.

www.ingramcontent.com/pod-product-compliance
Lightning Source LLC
Chambersburg PA
CBHW061725270326
41928CB00011B/2113